Labour Markets
The Economics of Work & Leisure

5th Edition

Peter Cramp

To my family

Thanks

Thanks to my friend and colleague Darren Poole,
who read the first draft of the first edition of this book
and made numerous helpful suggestions.

© Anforme Ltd 2011
ISBN 978-1-905504-68-8
Images supplied by Shutterstock.com

Anforme Ltd, Stocksfield Hall, Stocksfield, Northumberland NE43 7TN.

Typeset by George Wishart & Associates, Whitley Bay.
Printed by Potts Print (UK) Ltd.

Contents

Introduction 1

Section A: Labour Markets

Unit 1   The Supply of Labour 3

Unit 2   The Demand for Labour 11

Unit 3   Wage Determination in a Competitive Labour Market 16

Unit 4   Wage Differentials 20

Unit 5   The Role of Trade Unions 28

Unit 6   The Case of Monopsony 32

Unit 7   Government Intervention in Labour Markets 34

Unit 8   Unemployment and Labour Market Imperfections 38

Unit 9   Government Policies to Influence Productivity and Labour Mobility 44

Unit 10   The Flexibility of UK and EU Labour Markets 50

Unit 11   Ageing Populations in Developed Countries 56

Unit 12   The Distribution of Income and Wealth 60

Unit 13   Measurement of Inequality: the Lorenz Curve and the Gini Coefficient 64

Unit 14   Policy Issues associated with Poverty and Inequality 67

Section B: Leisure Markets

Unit 15   Market Structures 72

Unit 16   Holidays and Leisure Travel 79

Unit 17   Cinema Admissions 87

Unit 18   Spectator Sports 93

Unit 19   Television Broadcasting 102

Index 108

Introduction

Labour markets compared to markets for products and services

Labour is one of the four factors of production identified by economists. The others are land, capital and enterprise. These factors are combined to make goods (products) and services.

It is likely that before reading this book you will have spent some time studying market theory in relation to markets for goods and services. You will probably be familiar with the idea that in a perfectly competitive market the price of a good or service and the quantity of it traded are determined by the interaction of demand and supply. You will perhaps also know that imperfections in the market can change its outcome. An example of an imperfection is the presence of a monopolist, who is in a position to restrict supply in order to raise the price of his product. If the theory of perfect competition and monopoly is new to you, it may be helpful to read Unit 15 before studying the labour markets section of this book.

In your study of labour markets, you will have the opportunity to apply much of the economics that you have already learned. This is because in some regards a labour market is much like any other market. Indeed, this book begins with a look at the determinants of labour supply and demand. It then goes on to analyse, amongst other things, labour market imperfections. Trade unions sometimes seek to control the supply of labour in much the same way as a monopolist does the supply of a good or service. This forces up the wage. On the demand side, a sole buyer of a particular type of labour is called a monopsonist. The NHS has substantial monopsonistic power in the hiring of nurses, for example. Such power can be used to drive wages down.

In other respects, labour markets are very different from those for other services and products. One reason why the labour market is special is that the services of people are being traded. Men and women are not impassive in the same way that, say, a chocolate bar is! This makes labour markets more complex than other markets. For instance, it is possible that a labourer will intensify his efforts and become more productive if his wage increases. On the other hand, the chocolate bar is still the same chocolate bar after its price has increased.

The labour market can be argued to be more important than most other markets. Much of the national income is generated through the employment of labour (the rest of it is rewards to the other factors of production, namely land, capital and entrepreneurship). The labour market thus probably makes more difference to the living standards of a nation and to those of the individuals that compose it than any other market.

Defining labour markets

There are many labour markets which overlap. For example the market for labour in Liverpool is part of the North West's labour market, which in turn is part of the national labour market. In particular we will be concerned with:

Local labour markets which are particularly important in studying the differences in pay between different regions

and

Occupational labour markets in which we study the determinants of pay and employment levels in particular jobs. It may be more relevant to look at the national market for teachers than the market for teachers in York, for example. This is because few teachers limit their search for work to a particular city.

There will be times, however, when we will split the labour market up in other ways. One example would be the **labour market by gender** if we were concerned with the difference between male and female wages.

Finally, there will be times when we talk simply of *the* labour market. This would usually refer to the aggregate labour market at national level. We might look at the national labour market when studying the level of unemployment, for example.

Leisure markets

From an economic point of view, individuals have to make choices about how to spend their time. An hour of time can either be spent working or enjoying leisure and the opportunity cost of an hour's leisure time is the wage that could have been earned by working instead.

Accordingly, the concepts of work (and thus labour markets) and leisure are closely linked. Unit 1 of this book covers the choice between work and leisure time in more detail. This choice having been made, individuals must then decide how to use the leisure time that they have at their disposal. Leisure markets are those which provide activities for people to undertake during their leisure time or products for them to use. Examples of leisure markets include the markets for package holidays, air travel, spectator sports and television broadcasting, which are covered in Units 16 to 19 of this book.

The leisure sector of the economy is of great importance. Examples of this importance include: The significant effect of tourism on the balance of payments; the substantial number of people employed in leisure industries and the income generated by them; the environmental impact of some leisure industries.

The importance of the leisure sector has grown over time. This is largely because of a trend increase in income, combined with the fact that leisure activities tend to be income elastic (when income grows, demand for leisure activities grows more than proportionately). This is reflected in the change in the weights used to calculate the Consumer Prices Index, shown in the graph below. It is noticeable that categories associated with the leisure industry, such as recreation and culture and restaurants and hotels, have seen an increase in their weights. This indicates that they account for a greater proportion of household expenditure than previously.

CPI weights (parts per 1000)

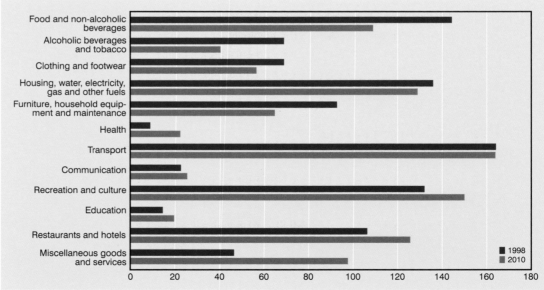

Source: Constructed using official CPI weights quoted in *Consumer Prices Index and Retail Prices Index: Updating Weights for 2010*, Sharne Bailey, Prices Division, Office for National Statistics

The Supply of Labour

Defining the labour supply (the working population)

The labour supply consists of all those who are economically active. An individual is economically active if he/she is participating in the labour market by either:

- Working or
- Actively seeking work at going wage rates.

The labour supply is also known as the **labour force** or **work force**. Another name still is the **working population**. A common mistake, to be avoided, is to treat the working population as consisting simply of those people that are actually working. It also includes those that are not in work but are actively seeking it. Those not in work but currently seeking it are defined as being **unemployed**.

Economic inactivity

The economically inactive are neither in work nor seeking it. By definition, these sections of the population are not part of the labour supply.

One such section is those not of a working age. The **population of working age** until recently referred to men between 16 and 65 and women between 16 and 60. However, females will soon not receive the state pension until they are 65. This change is being phased in over time and began in 2010. Furthermore, the state pension age for both males and females is scheduled to rise gradually to stand at 68 for all citizens by the year 2046.

There are also a number of groups that are of a working age but do not participate in the labour market. These groups include full-time students, housewives, prisoners and the severely disabled. Figure 1.1 offers more detail on economic activity and inactivity.

Participation ratios (activity rates)

There are many occasions on which it is useful for economists to measure the percentage of a particular group which is economically active. For example:

▶ The **participation ratio** is usually calculated as the percentage of the population of working age that is economically active: (labour supply/population of working age) x 100.

▶ The **female participation ratio** is then the female labour supply taken as a percentage of the female population of working age: (female labour supply/female population of working age) x 100.

It should immediately be apparent that we can calculate a participation ratio for any group within the labour market. Check that you are able to define the participation ratio for men between the ages of 16 and 25.

It is important to be aware that participation ratios are sometimes also referred to as **activity rates** or **ratios**. The other side of the coin is **inactivity rates**. By definition, the activity rate and inactivity rate for any group must sum to 100%.

Figure 1.1: Economic activity (left hand side) and inactivity (right hand side)

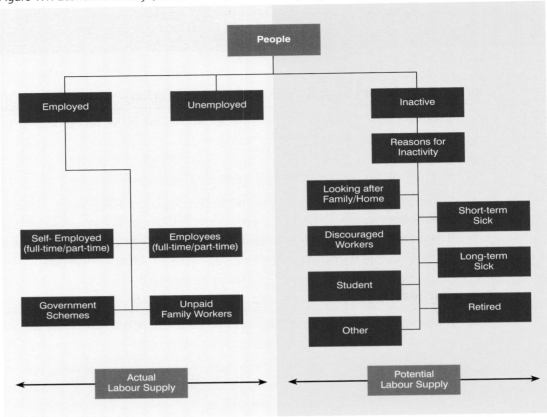

Source: Office for National Statistics, Labour Market Review 2006

The structure of labour supply

The structure of labour supply refers to the size and the composition of the workforce. There are two factors which determine the structure of labour supply. These are:

- Demographics (population factors) and
- Participation ratios

Thus the size of the workforce depends on the size of the population of working age (15-60/65) and on the percentage of those of a working age who choose to be economically active.

Similarly, the age composition of the workforce depends on how many people there are in the country in each age grouping and the participation ratio amongst each age group. In exactly the same way, the composition of labour supply by gender depends on the populations of men and women of a working age and the relative male and female participation ratios.

The size of the workforce

▶ *Demographics.* Other things being equal, the larger the population, the larger the working population too. The UK population is increasing over time and for the first time topped 60 million in 2006. This is largely due to migration. Also crucial is the age distribution of the population. This is currently the focus of much attention because a gradual ageing of the population is occurring such that in the future a greater proportion of the population will not be of working age. The labour supply will be smaller as a result. This problem is sometimes known as the **demographic timebomb** and is discussed in depth in Unit 11.

▶ *Participation ratios.* A higher participation ratio makes for a larger working population. Factors which affect participation ratios are many and varied. They include: 1. *Government policy.* This frequently impacts on the size of the working population. We have noted already the raising of the retirement age which will serve to increase the working population. Government initiatives to encourage more females to work, such as measures to increase the availability of childcare, do likewise. On the other hand, the working population is lowered by attempts to encourage students beyond the age of 16 to remain in full time education. 2. *The state of the economy.* When the economy is struggling some potential workers may become disillusioned and leave the labour market. 3. *Social trends.* These include changing social attitudes towards women and their participation in the labour market.

The size of the labour force can be obtained from the information in Table 1.1. The final column headed 'all aged 16 and over' shows the male and female labour forces in particular years. The total labour force for any year can be found by adding the male and female labour forces for that year. This method has been used to derive Table 1.2, which shows that the labour force has grown significantly since 1971 and is forecast to grow further by 2020. From Table 1.1, it would appear that the main source of this growth is an increase in the female labour supply. A higher female participation rate may be the reason for this.

Table 1.1: Labour force by gender and age (millions)

United Kingdom						65 and	All aged 16
	16-24	25-44	45-54	55-59	60-64	over	and over
Males							
1971	3.0	6.5	3.2	1.5	1.3	0.6	16.0
1981	3.2	7.1	3.0	1.4	1.0	0.3	16.0
1991	3.1	8.1	3.0	1.1	0.8	0.3	16.4
2001	2.4	7.9	3.4	1.2	0.7	0.3	15.9
2011*	2.6	7.6	3.8	1.3	1.0	0.4	16.7
2020*	2.3	7.7	3.8	1.7	1.1	0.5	17.1
Females							
1971	2.3	3.5	2.1	0.9	0.5	0.3	10.0
1981	2.7	4.6	2.1	0.9	0.4	0.2	10.9
1991	2.6	6.1	2.4	0.8	0.3	0.2	12.4
2001	2.1	6.7	3.0	1.0	0.4	0.2	13.3
2011*	2.6	7.6	3.8	1.4	1.0	0.4	16.8
2020*	2.4	7.7	3.8	1.7	1.1	0.5	17.1

Source: Office for National Statistics data, primarily Labour Force Projections 2006-2020 (Vassilis Madouros, January 2006). *Projections

Table 1.2: Labour force (millions)

Labour Force	
1971	26.0
1981	26.9
1991	28.8
2001	29.2
2011*	33.5
2020*	34.2

Source: Derived from Table 1.1. *Projections

A much larger proportion of the working population will be aged over 50 in 2020.

The age profile of the working population

Figure 1.2: The age profile of the male working population

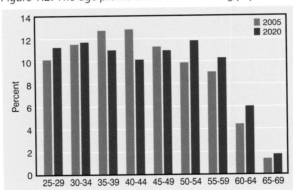

Source: Office for National Statistics Labour Force Projections 2006–2020
(Vassillis Madouros)

Data on the age profile of the working population can be found in Table 1.1 and Figure 1.2. This age profile is determined by:

▶ *Demographics.* An important factor in this section is the ageing of the population, as discussed in the previous section. The projections in Figure 1.2 suggest that a much larger proportion of the working population will be aged 50 and above in 2020 than was the case in 2005.

▶ *Participation ratios.* For example, an increased proportion of **young people remaining in further education** after the age of 16 reduces participation ratios amongst young people and by implication lessens the proportion of the labour force who are young. **Increased female participation** changes the age profile of the working population, because most of the increased participation is occurring amongst women of a child bearing age. An inspection of Table 1.1 reveals that the female labour force between the ages of 25 and 44 came close to doubling over the period 1971-2001.

The sex distribution of the working population

The sex distribution of the working population is determined by:

▶ *Demographics.* The relevant factor here is the relative sizes of the male and female populations of working age.

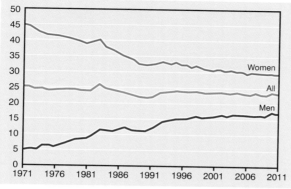

Figure 1.3: Inactivity rates, ages 16-64, UK (%)

Source: Office for National Statistics, Social Trends 41, 2011 Edition

▶ *Participation ratios.* Also important is the relative participation ratios of males and females. The clearest trend in this area is currently towards increased female participation in the labour market, especially amongst women of a child bearing age. This is shown in Figure 1.3 as a falling inactivity rate amongst women. The reasons are examined in the next sub-section. Male participation ratios have fallen over time as inactivity has increased.

Explaining participation ratios

Students of labour markets need to be able to explain different participation rates amongst different groups and changes in participation ratios over time.

Female participation ratios

Factors which help to explain the rising female participation ratio include:

▶ Government policy (discussed in the section on the size of the working population).

▶ Social trends (also discussed in the section on the size of the working population).

▶ The changing structure of the economy. This is presenting new opportunities to females, encouraging greater participation. As the economy shifts towards the service sector, the demand for female labour tends to increase. Employers often view female labour as better suited to much of the work in this sector. Also, employers increasingly ask that employees adapt to flexible working practices with regard to part time employment and the timing of hours worked. This may suit well those women that wish to combine work and family commitments.

Male participation ratios

Male participation ratios have fallen since 1971, when the rate was 95%, to 83% in 2011. This is partly as a result of there being fewer labour market opportunities for males as a result of the restructuring of the economy towards the service sector. A reduction in opportunities can lead to workers becoming discouraged and leaving the labour market altogether.

Participation ratios of different ethnic groups

The reasons for varying activity rates amongst different ethnic groups are likely to centre on differing labour market opportunities and on cultural factors. Generalisations are difficult to make because the cultural factors may vary greatly from group to group. A specific example is that the participation ratio amongst young Chinese males is very low due to the importance attached to full-time education.

The primary reason for the fact that participation ratios amongst whites are higher than those for any other ethnic group is likely to be the greater labour market opportunities available to whites. Unemployment is lower for whites than for other groups (see Unit 8) and rates of pay higher (see Unit 4). A relative lack of labour market opportunities for minority ethnic groups may cause some members of them to become discouraged and leave the workforce.

Table 1.3: Economic activity rate by ethnic group (UK, Quarter 2 2009, not seasonally adjusted)

	Men (%)	Women %	All (%)
White British	70	57	63
Other White	76	62	69
Mixed	72	63	67
Indian	77	58	68
Pakistani	72	34	54
Bangladeshi	75	31	54
Other Asian	75	59	66
Black Caribbean	69	66	68
Black African	71	56	63
Other Black	Unavailable	47	52
Chinese	72	57	60
Other ethnic group	72	54	63

Source: Derived using figures from Office for National Statistics, Social Trends 41, 2011 edition

Participation ratios of people with disabilities

The participation ratios of people with disabilities are lower than those of people without disabilities. The two main reasons for this are that some disabilities are so severe as to make it difficult or even impossible to be economically active and that the labour market opportunities available to people with disabilities may be fewer. This may be due to discrimination, even though this is illegal.

Table 1.4: Activity rates for the disabled

	Men		Women		All	
	Disabled	Not Disabled	Disabled	Not Disabled	Disabled	Not Disabled
Activity rate (%)	57	90	49	78	53	85

Source: ONS, Labour Force Survey/Social Trends 34, 2004 edition

The individual's choice between work and leisure

The alternative to working is to enjoy leisure time. For each hour that an individual works, he foregoes an hour of leisure. An hour of leisure is therefore the **opportunity cost** of the decision to supply an hour of labour, where opportunity cost is defined as the cost of making a decision expressed in terms of the next best alternative foregone. If an hour of leisure is chosen instead, the opportunity cost is the wage foregone.

The individual's labour supply curve: income and substitution effects

In drawing the individual's labour supply curve real wages are used rather than nominal. This is because the real wage is the true measure of the reward from an hour's labour and we would expect this to be the basis of the labour supply decision.

A possible shape for the individual's labour supply curve is shown in Figure 1.4. It probably looks most unlike other supply curves that you have seen. This is because it is commonly held that at high wage levels an increase in the wage will actually lead to a reduction in the hours of labour supplied, giving rise to a backward bending labour supply curve.

Why should this be so? The effect of a change in wage on an individual's labour supply can be divided into two components: the **substitution and income effects**. If wages rise, leisure becomes relatively more

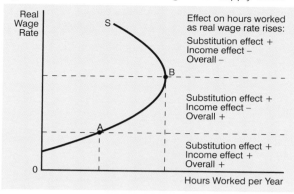

Figure 1.4: The backward bending labour supply curve

expensive (it has a higher opportunity cost). Thus there will be a tendency to substitute extra hours of work, replacing hours of leisure. The substitution effect always works in this way.

The direction of the income effect is less clear. If his wage rises the worker's income at current hours worked has risen. This boost to income might encourage extra work and typically does for those whose wages are low. However, those with higher wages may find that an increase in wages allows them to reach a **target income** by working fewer hours. Thus, in Figure 1.4 the income effect is shown as negative beyond point A (working against the substitution effect) and sufficiently strong to lead to fewer hours being worked overall beyond point B. According to this analysis, leisure is a luxury good, more affordable to those with higher wages.

The supply curve of labour to an industry

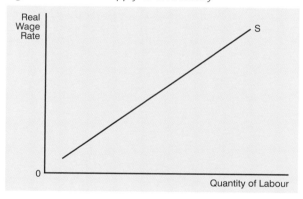

Figure 1.5: Labour supply to an industry

A change in the wage level in an industry causes a movement along its labour supply curve.

An industry's labour supply curve is generally upward sloping, left to right (see Figure 1.5). This implies that an increased real wage causes an extension of supply despite the fact that the labour supply curves of individual workers already in the industry may be backward bending. This is because a higher wage is likely to attract new workers into the industry. These workers are drawn largely from those currently working in other areas. For example, an increase in the wages of nurses may bring back many that have trained as nurses but are now working elsewhere (or are economically inactive).

The **elasticity of labour supply** measures the responsiveness of labour supply to a change in the real wage and varies from industry to industry. In general terms, elasticity of labour supply for an industry depends on:

▶ *The nature of the skill required in the job.* Jobs which require skills which are very specific to the job are less likely to attract workers from other industries when the real wage rises. This is simply because there are fewer worker in other industries that possess the relevant skills. Labour supply thus tends to be inelastic.

▶ *The length of the training period.* Jobs where the training period is lengthy tend to have low elasticities of labour supply. Workers are less willing to move into the industry in response to an increase in real wage because of the length of the training period. Furthermore, any workers who are attracted into the industry by a higher wage will take a long time to come through fully qualified. Doctors are a good example of this.

▶ *Vocation.* Jobs which have a vocational element tend to have low elasticities of labour supply. For teachers, nurses and the clergy, for example, the reward from work is not entirely monetary and this dampens the supply response to a change in the real wage.

▶ *Time span under consideration.* When the real wage in an industry changes it takes time for workers to adjust their labour supply decisions. The response to a wage change is thus small the day after the change occurs, but elasticity will be greater after a month and still greater after a year. Reasons for this include the notice which must be given before leaving one job for another and the training required in some jobs.

Shifts of the labour supply curve

A change in any factor which affects the labour supply to an industry apart from the wage level itself will result in a shift of the supply curve. Such factors include:

▶ *An increase in the working population.* Other things being equal, when the economy's labour force changes, so will the labour supply to each industry. If there are more workers in the economy there are likely to be more workers in each industry too.

▶ *Changed working conditions and levels of non-monetary rewards in the industry.* For example, improved working conditions will attract new workers to the industry.

▶ *Changed wage levels and working conditions in other industries.* The relative attractiveness of working in other industries will affect the labour supply to any particular industry.

▶ *A change in the value placed on leisure time.* If the value which people attach to leisure increases then people are less likely to work at any given wage rate and labour supply will be lowered.

Unit 2

The Demand for Labour

Labour as a derived demand

The demand for labour is a derived demand. Employers do not hire workers because they enjoy doing so, in the way that a consumer buys a bar of chocolate because of the utility that eating it brings. Employers hire workers because doing so enables the company to make products or offer services which can be sold at a profit.

This is clearly only possible so long as a demand for the product or service exists. In other words, the demand for a particular type of labour is derived from the demand for the product or service that the labour produces. For example, there is only a demand for lawyers because there is also a demand for legal services.

The UK's changing employment pattern

Because labour is a derived demand, the pattern of employment is dictated largely by the pattern of demand for goods and services. The pattern of demand for UK goods and services has changed dramatically in recent decades. This **structural change** in the economy is reflected in a change in the pattern of employment as shown in Figure 2.1.

Figure 2.1: UK employment in industry

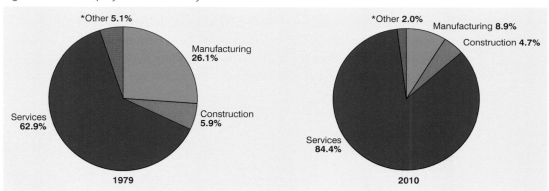

Source: Created using data from Office for National Statistics, Social Trends 41, 2011 edition   *Including agriculture and fishing

The broad structure of the economy can be defined by dividing it into four sectors:

▶ The primary sector covers the extraction of raw materials from the natural environment, together with the growth of food.

▶ The secondary sector combines raw materials with other factors of production in order to produce goods.

▶ The tertiary sector provides services.

▶ The quaternary sector provides information services. Internet services are an example.

The nature of the structural change in the UK economy and hence in the derived demand for labour is that there is less output and employment in the primary and secondary sectors and more in the tertiary and quaternary sectors. Note that in 1979, 26.1% of UK employment was in manufacturing. By 2010 this figure was just 8.9%. Meanwhile employment in services rose from 62.9% of the total to 84.4%. The majority of the additional service sector jobs have been created in hotels and restaurants and finance and business services.

Another striking feature of changing employment patterns is the explosion of employment in IT products and related services. There were 855,000 people being employed in this field in the UK by Spring 2000. This represents a 45% increase on just five years earlier.

It is important to be aware of some of the reasons for this change in the structure of output and employment. They include:

▶ International competition. Sectors of the economy such as manufacturing are labour intensive. Competition from countries with plentiful supplies of cheap labour has been difficult for UK industry to withstand. Much of this competition has come from newly industrialised countries (NICs) which have pursued industrialisation as part of their development strategies.

▶ Rising incomes which have raised the demand for services. This demand is elastic with respect to income.

▶ Technological advance has led to the rapid development of the quaternary sector.

Demand curves for labour (marginal productivity theory)

A demand curve for labour is a relationship between the real wage in a labour market and the quantity of labour demanded over a given time period. As with any demand curve, it is drawn on the assumption that all other determinants of demand are held constant. Here this includes the quantities and prices of other inputs to the production process, such as capital. This means that the labour demand curve is drawn for the **short run**, which is defined as the period in which at least one factor of production is fixed in quantity.

In the short run, the **law of diminishing marginal returns** applies. Output can only be increased by adding more of a variable input (labour) to the existing stock of fixed factors (including capital). Initially the **marginal physical product** (**MPP**) of labour increases, as each worker adds more to output than the previous worker did. This is due to the scope for gains from specialisation as more division of labour is possible when there are more workers. However, there must come a point at which the gains from specialisation begin to be exhausted and an extra worker has a smaller MPP than the previous worker.

Changing employment patterns have seen an explosion of employment in IT products and related services.

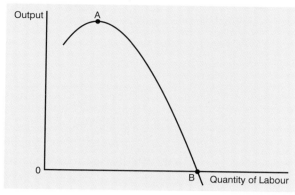

Figure 2.2: Marginal Physical Product

Diminishing marginal returns are said to set in at this point (point A). This suggests a pattern of MPP as illustrated in Figure 2.2. As shown, there may even come a point at which a worker will have a negative MPP, and his employment will reduce total output (point B).

More important than marginal physical product to the firm is the addition to its revenue from employing an extra worker. This is known as a worker's **marginal revenue product** (**MRP**). It is calculated by multiplying the worker's marginal physical product by the **marginal revenue** (**MR**) brought in from the sale of each extra unit:

$$MRP = MPP \times MR$$

If we assume that the firm's product is sold in a perfectly competitive market, then the firm becomes a **price-taker** and the price of its product is not reduced when extra units of output are sold. Thus the marginal revenue from the sale of an extra unit is simply the price (P) and then:

$$MRP = MPP \times P$$

The MRP curve can now be drawn as the same basic shape as the MPP curve (see Figure 2.2), because it is the MPP curve multiplied by a constant factor (the price).

Suppose that an extra worker adds 10 units of output a week of a product which is sold for £10 in a perfectly competitive market. This worker's marginal revenue product is £100.

Now we assume further that the labour market is perfectly competitive, so that no individual firm can influence the wage, but must hire workers at the market wage (W). If the weekly wage set in the market is less than £100, the firm will find it profitable to employ this worker. This is because the additional revenue generated by the worker exceeds the cost of hiring him. However, if the market wage is above £100 it will not be profitable to hire the worker. Extra workers will be employed so long as:

$$MRP > W$$

The application of the rule can be seen in Figure 2.3. If the wage is W_1, all workers prior to the Q_1th worker have marginal revenue products in excess of the wage and are profitable to hire, but none beyond it. Q_1 workers are therefore hired if the market wage is W_1. By similar reasoning, Q_2 workers are hired if the wage rate is W_2 and so on. Thus the MRP curve also gives the relationship between the market wage and the quantity of labour hired and thus is the labour demand curve.

Figure 2.3 Marginal revenue product and labour demand

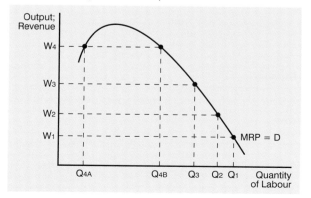

One proviso to this conclusion is that for some wage levels, the MRP will be equal to the wage at more than one employment level (see W_4 for example). Here it is profitable to employ to the second point where the wage equals the MRP. Note that all workers between Q_{4A} and Q_{4B} have MRPs in excess of the wage and hence are profitable to employ. Because of this Q_{4B} workers are employed and the labour demand curve is the downward sloping section of the MRP curve.

The assumptions of marginal revenue productivity theory

Implicit in the theory discussed above are the following assumptions:

▶ *All factors of production other than labour are fixed in quantity* (discussed in the section headed Demand curves for labour)

▶ *Workers are homogeneous* and have the same level of aptitude for the job. It does not matter who the 15th worker is, he will have the same marginal product whoever he is. Equally, the 15th worker has the same aptitude as the 14th worker. If he has a lower marginal product this is simply because an increased amount of labour is now combined with a fixed stock of capital. The assumption that labour is homogeneous is clearly not realistic but is a necessary simplification. It does not alter the fact that the MRP curve as it is drawn in Figure 2.3 does broadly describe what happens in the real world when increasing quantities of labour are added to a fixed stock of capital.

▶ *The labour market is perfectly competitive.* This assumption can later be relaxed in order to give the theory more explanatory power in real world situations where trade unions and powerful employers operate, and governments intervene in the market (see Units 5-7).

▶ *A perfectly competitive product market* is often, but not always, assumed (see *Demand curves for labour* section).

It is also worth noting at this point that marginal revenue product can be very difficult to measure for employers and, indeed, economists. This is especially so where the output in question is a service, or where the output is not marketed (as in the case of state education or health care).

Shifts of the labour demand curve

When any factor which affects labour demand other than the wage itself changes, the demand curve shifts. Factors that would cause such a shift include:

▶ *A change in the price of the final product that labour makes.* This means that the marginal physical product that each worker produces is worth either more or less when it is sold. If the marginal revenue product of each worker increases, demand for labour shifts right.

▶ *Changes in demand for the final product.* Because labour is a derived demand, a change in the demand for the final product results in a change in the demand for labour.

▶ *Changes to labour productivity.* These affect the marginal physical and revenue products of labour. Higher marginal revenue product would result in higher labour demand.

▶ *Changes in the price of capital.* In the long run, the production process can employ varying quantities of capital and other factors of production. Capital can be used as a substitute for labour in the production process. Other things being equal, it is to be expected that a fall in the price of capital will lead to more of it being employed and less labour. This results in the labour demand curve shifting to the left.

The elasticity of demand for labour

The elasticity of demand for labour measures the responsiveness of labour demand to a change in the real wage rate. Its determinants include:

▶ *The ease of substitution of capital for labour and vice-versa.* This influences the long run response to a change in the relative price of labour to capital (see previous section).

▶ *The time span under consideration.* The substitution of capital for labour is easier as time goes

Wage increases feed through to price increases, making labour demand more elastic.

on following an increase in the relative price of labour, causing long run elasticity to be greater than short run.

▶ *Elasticity of demand for the product.* Wage increases feed through to price increases (directly if a mark-up pricing policy is followed). Price increases lead to a contraction of demand for the product and hence a contraction of the derived demand for labour. The more elastic is product demand, the greater will be the contraction of demand both for the product and for labour. This serves to make labour demand more elastic.

▶ *The proportion of labour to total cost.* If labour is an insignificant fraction of total costs, any increase in wages is unlikely to have a significant effect on labour demand, leading to a lower elasticity of labour demand.

Unit 3
Wage Determination in a Competitive Labour Market

A perfectly competitive labour market

A fully competitive labour market is one in which the conditions listed below exist. Many of these have been stated in the derivation of the labour supply and demand curves in the previous two units.

▶ There are many suppliers of labour to the market (potential workers) and many hirers of labour (employers). Each of these individual agents is small in relation to the overall market.

▶ There is homogeneity of labour.

▶ All participants in the market enjoy perfect knowledge of the market conditions.

▶ The above conditions ensure that each market participant is a 'wage-taker' and is not able to exercise any power over the market. Note that an employer has no incentive to offer above the 'going rate' for the job if all workers are homogeneous. Equally, no individual worker could demand more than the market wage, because employers know that other workers with the same skills are available.

▶ There is no government intervention in the labour market.

It is expected that you will recognise in the above the application of the conditions of perfect competition that you have previously studied with regard to product markets.

As with fully competitive product markets, fully competitive labour markets do not exist in reality. There is no market in which labour is perfectly homogeneous. In many markets there are powerful employers on the demand side and trade unions controlling the supply of labour too. Knowledge is unlikely to be perfect.

This said, the perfectly competitive labour market is a satisfactory model for analysing labour markets where these conditions exist approximately. Also, it is an important reference point for understanding the outcome of markets where the conditions differ substantially from those outlined above.

Equilibrium in a perfectly competitive labour market

Having derived labour demand and supply curves for an industry in the previous two units, we can now identify the equilibrium wage and employment levels. A perfectly competitive labour market will clear at the wage and employment levels indicated in Figure 3.1(a).

Figure 3.1(b) illustrates the significance of this for an individual firm in the industry. As a wage-taker, the firm must accept the wage set by the industry. In the face of a declining marginal revenue product (MRP) as more workers are employed, it will employ workers only as long as MRP exceeds the wage.

Figure 3.1: Wage determination in a competitive market

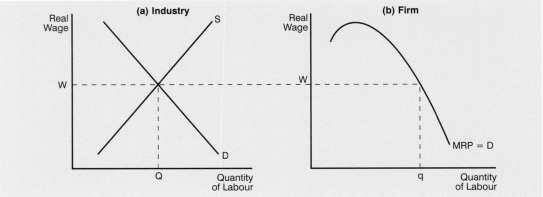

Changes to market equilibrium

Along the length of the supply and demand curves in Figure 3.1 all variables besides the wage are held constant. Changes to other variables affecting labour supply and demand decisions will shift the relevant curve and result in a change of equilibrium.

For a list of factors which would shift the labour supply curve see Unit 1. A similar list for labour demand is in Unit 2.

David Ricardo's theory of economic rent

The theory of economic rent distinguishes two separate elements in the payment made to a factor of production:

▶ The **transfer earnings** of a factor are the minimum payment required to keep a factor in its present use (the **opportunity cost** of its present use).

▶ **Economic rent** is any payment made to a factor over and above its transfer earnings.

For example, a worker who earns £500 per week, but could only earn £350 in his/her next best paid occupation has transfer earnings of £350 and receives economic rent of £150. If his/her weekly wage was increased to £600, all other things being equal, his/her transfer earnings would be unchanged but his/her economic rent would rise to £250.

We are primarily concerned here with the payment to labour (wages), but payments to other factors of production could be analysed in the same way. For example, profit (the return to entrepreneurship) is split into two components. Normal profit represents the transfer earnings of the entrepreneur and supernormal profits the economic rent.

In diagrammatical terms any given point on the supply curve represents the wage which is necessary to keep the corresponding number of workers in this market. The area under the supply curve is therefore transfer earnings. The area above the supply curve represents payments in excess of transfer earnings and is economic rent (see Figure 3.2).

Figure 3.2: Economic rent and transfer earnings

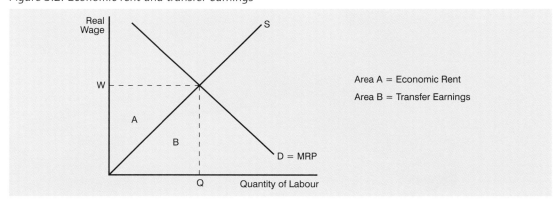

The main influence on the relative levels of economic rent and transfer earnings is the elasticity of labour supply to the market. Students can confirm this by rotating the supply curve around the equilibrium point as shown in Figure 3.3. The two supply curves give the same total payment to labour, but for the more inelastic supply curve more of this represents economic rent.

To understand this, consider a market where labour supply is highly inelastic. The priesthood, for example, is likely to be one such market given the vocational nature of the job. Most priests would be willing to work in their job for very low wages. Much of the wage which they are paid is thus economic rent. Footballers

Figure 3.3: Inelastic labour supply leads to high levels of economic rent

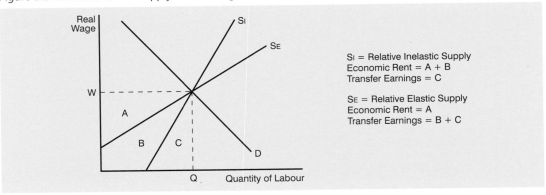

are another case in point. Footballers with the skills to play in the Premiership are in short supply. The extremely high wages on offer have not produced a flood of players of the calibre required; supply is clearly inelastic. Equally, very few Premiership footballers would be working in other occupations if their salaries as footballers were substantially lower. It is thus apparent that economic rent is high.

Where supply is totally inelastic, those working in the labour market would do so even if the wage were zero. The entire payment to labour is economic rent (see Figure 3.4a). However, if labour supply is perfectly elastic the entire payment is transfer earnings (see Figure 3.4b). Any reduction in wage levels in the market would cause all workers to leave the market.

Markets with time lags

One of the functions of wages is to act as a signal for allocating labour resources. For instance, an increase in the wage should serve to attract more workers into the market from elsewhere.

Consider the case of an increase in demand for accountants leading to an increase in their wages. This should attract extra workers to the profession, generating the extension of supply that will bring about a new equilibrium.

The supply of accountants is likely to be inelastic in the short run leading to increases in salary which represent extra economic rent.

Figure 3.4: Economic rent and transfer earnings under extreme elasticity conditions

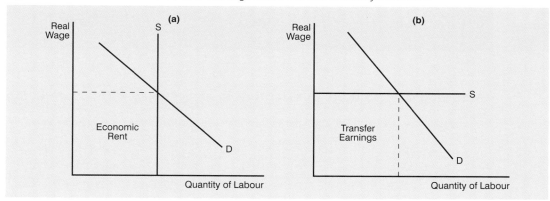

A problem here is that the training period for accountants is lengthy. Supply is likely to be inelastic in the short run, although it will extend in the long term. During the interim period, a shortage of accountants will exist. On a temporary basis, this will probably enable them to enjoy an artificially high salary. This increase in salary represents extra economic rent which will be lost once enough time has elapsed for new accountants to be trained. Temporary economic rent of this kind is called **quasi-rent**.

In this example, the interim period is likely to be several years. This leads to a further problem for the smooth working of the market. Market conditions are likely to change again before the newly trained accountants enter the market.

Unit 4

Wage Differentials

There would be no wage differentials in an economy with a perfect labour market

Recall the characteristics of a perfectly competitive labour market outlined in Unit 3.

Now suppose that the labour market in question is not a labour market for a particular occupation but is the labour market for the whole economy. The condition that workers are homogeneous must now be taken to mean that all workers are equally adept at performing all jobs in the economy. There would be no barrier preventing a brick layer becoming a pilot, for example.

The implication of this is that **perfect mobility** of labour between occupations exists. If pilots get paid more than bricklayers, then bricklayers will leave their occupation to become pilots. The resulting reduction in the supply of bricklayers and increase in the supply of pilots will reduce the wage differential between the two occupations. The process will continue until the wage for bricklayers and pilots is equal.

The perfect labour market also possesses the characteristic of perfect geographical mobility of labour. If wages are higher in the south of the country than the north, then workers will migrate from the north to the south to take advantage of this. Again, the process will continue until the differential is removed.

It is clear that if the labour market were perfectly competitive across the whole economy then there would be no wage differentials. That large wage differentials *do* exist and that the labour market is *not* perfectly competitive is equally clear. However, the model of the perfectly competitive labour market helps us to understand the wage differentials that do exist. Their causes must be imperfections in the labour market. Identifying these imperfections enables us to understand why wages differ.

Why do wage rates differ?

As explained above, wage differentials can be attributed to labour market imperfections, given that all wages would be equal in a perfect labour market. Labour market imperfections include:

▶ *Each worker is unique* (i.e. labour is not homogeneous), with a unique set of characteristics in terms of: age, sex, ethnic background, education, training, work experience, personality and so on. These differing characteristics can lead to wage differentials through one or more of three sources:

- Differing marginal revenue products and therefore differing demands for different types of labour.
- Different supplies of different types of labour.
- Discrimination, despite anti-discrimination laws such as the 1976 Race Relations Act. Also, the Commission for Racial Equality teaches organisations how not to discriminate on racial grounds. The Equal Pay Act has established the principle that those doing work of 'comparable worth' should receive equal pay. This principle has been applied in cases brought on the grounds of both racial and sexual discrimination.

▶ *Market forces will tend to equalise net benefits to workers rather than net wages.* In the theory of the labour market outlined so far, wages are the only signal for the allocation of labour resources. In reality, individuals and firms base their supply and demand decisions on more than the basic wage level. Workers, for example, often receive rewards other than the wage. These range from material perks such as a company car to the vocational satisfaction enjoyed in jobs such as health care. On the other hand there may be unattractive aspects of working in some occupations, such as danger, high stress levels or an unpleasant working environment. Other things being equal, unpleasant jobs will have to pay more than pleasant jobs (the extra is sometimes termed a '**compensating differential**').

▶ *Labour is not perfectly mobile.* There are a number of reasons for this. These include:

- Occupational mobility may be limited by lack of skills or aptitude to acquire skills.
- Geographical mobility may be limited because many people may not wish to (or be able to afford to) move to another area in search of work.
- Both occupational and geographical mobility may be limited because workers do not enjoy perfect knowledge of job opportunities.

▶ *Lack of competition on the supply side of the labour market due to trade unions.* Trade unions enable workers to bargain as a collective unit rather than individually. This reduces competition in labour supply, with trade unions able deliberately to restrict the supply of labour in order to raise wages. The strength of trade unions differs from one occupation to another. See Unit 5 for more detail on trade unions.

▶ *Lack of competition on the demand side of the labour market due to powerful (monopsonist) employers.* An employer has monopsonist power if he accounts for a large enough share of employment in a particular labour market to be able to set his own wage rather than employ at the 'going rate' set in a competitive market. Such employers may use their power to drive down wages. See Unit 6 for further details on monopsonist employers.

It is important to be able to apply these ideas to explain wage differentials in a variety of contexts, including differentials between: males and females, different occupations, different geographical regions and different ethnic groupings. All of these areas are explored here, with male-female wage differentials treated as a detailed case-study accompanied by relevant data.

Examples

(i) Why do males get paid more than females?

Table 4.1 shows data on the difference between median hourly pay for males and females. Notable features of the data include:

- There is a significant gender pay gap, with median hourly pay for men exceeding that of women by 10.2% in 2010.
- The gender pay gap is narrowing over time, having stood at 17.4% in 1997.
- The gender pay gap varies significantly between different occupations, and in some jobs female median pay is higher than for males. For example, female median pay amongst company secretaries exceeds male median pay by 41.8%.

Specific explanations of male-female wage differentials include:

▶ Females, on average, have a lower degree of **attachment to the labour force** than men. Women are more likely than men to move in and out of the labour force, with many taking substantial career breaks in order to raise children. Time spent out of the labour force means a loss of valuable experience and therefore lower marginal revenue productivity.

Figure 4.1 shows that women with two children earn substantially less over their lifetime than a childless woman. The effect is greatest for the low-skilled. This is likely to be because more highly skilled women are better able to regain their place in the labour market following maternity, due to the value placed by employers on such skills.

▶ The age at which women tend not to be economically active due to child-bearing is just the age at which most progress up the career ladder is made by those with greater attachment to the labour force. Thus it is not just the loss of experience that damages marginal revenue productivity and wage earning potential, but the timing of that loss of experience.

Table 4.1: The gender pay gap

The gap in median hourly pay has narrowed

1997	1998	1999	2000	2001	2002	2003	2004	2005	2006	2007	2008	2009	2010
17.4%	17.4%	16.4%	16.3%	16.4%	15.5%	14.6%	14.5%	13.0%	12.6%	12.4%	12.6%	12.2%	10.2%

How much men and women get paid for selected jobs – gaps in full-time median hourly pay

	Men	Women	Gap
Metal making and treating process operatives	£11.29	£5.80	48.6%
Brokers	£28.75	£16.55	42.4%
Doctors	£35.45	£25.35	28.5%
Lawyers	£28.45	£21.75	23.6%
Director of major organisation	£49.70	£38.95	21.6%
All full-time jobs	£13.01	£11.68	10.2%
Secondary school teachers	£22.94	£21.36	6.9%
Physiotherapists	£15.59	£15.59	0%
Journalists and editors	£15.60	£15.71	-0.7%
Social workers	£16.55	£16.78	-1.4%
Company secretaries	£9.75	£13.83	-41.8%

Source: www.guardian.co.uk, International Women's Day: the pay gap between men and women for your job (8 March 2011)

Figure 4.1: Lifetime earnings of men, childless women and women with two children

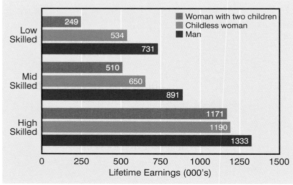

Source: Women's Incomes Over Their Lifetimes (Cabinet Office)

▶ The older age groups in today's labour force were educated at a time when females enjoyed fewer educational opportunities than males and did not on average attain as high a level of qualification as men.

This can help to explain the data shown in Figure 4.2, where the gender pay gap is at its greatest for 50-59 year olds. It is also the case that for the 22-29 age bracket, the gender gap actually favours females. This may reflect the fact that female educational attainment now exceeds that of males at GCSE, A Level and degree Level. This is confirmed to be the case for GCSE level by Figure 4.3. The gender pay gap is likely to narrow further over time as retiring workers continue to be replaced by those who have been recently educated.

It must be noted, however, that educational attainment is not the only explanation of the pattern seen in Figure 4.2. Patterns of pay are also influenced by many other factors, including the effect of experience on marginal revenue productivity. The large pay gap in favour of males from the age of 40 upwards is caused

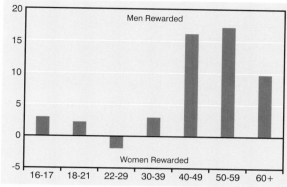

Figure 4.2: Gender pay difference by age group (%)

Source: ONS Economic and Labour Market Review, March 2011-07-24

Figure 4.3: Percentage of boys and girls achieving 5 or more GCSEs, grade A*-C

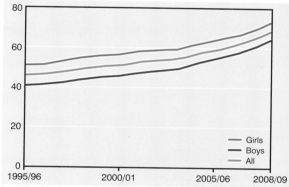

Source: Office for National Statistics, Social Trends 41, 2011 Edition

partly by loss of experience for females due to lower degree of attachment to the labour force in child-bearing years (see previous point for further detail).

► There is a concentration of female labour in certain occupations where, for various reasons, lower wages are paid. Figure 4.4 shows that the majority of labour is female in many low paid occupations.

It should be noted that concentrations of female labour exist in:

► Part-time work, which is especially attractive to women who wish to combine work and family commitments. It is obvious that part-time workers are likely to get paid less in total than full-time workers because they work fewer hours. Figure 4.5 shows that the *hourly* wage for female and male part-time workers is fairly similar for lower paid groups in the income distribution.

► Work in the service sector. Some, but not all, work in the service sector is undemanding in terms of the skill level required.

Figure 4.4: Proportion of male and female employees in low-paying occupations, UK, 2008 (%)

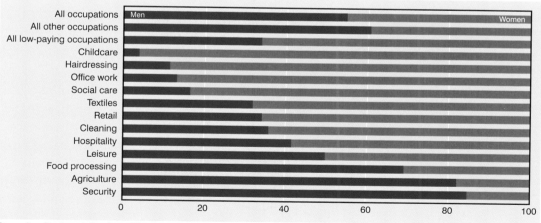

Source: Low Pay Commission, Annual Report on the Minimum Wage, 2009

► Work in the public sector. Around two-thirds of public sector employees are female. The state is a near monopsonist employer of some types of labour, which serves to hold wages down. Governments have been especially keen to control public sector pay as a counter-inflationary policy and to constrain the budget deficit.

► Vocational work. Jobs which carry a great deal of satisfaction tend to carry lower pay as job satisfaction increases labour supply at any given wage rate. A concentration of female labour in occupations such as nursing is therefore an explanation of the gender pay gap.

▶ Occupations where union density (see Unit 5) is low. This reduces the power of unions to raise wages. There is a clear over-lap here with the point that female labour is concentrated in part-time work and service sector work. The diffuse nature of work in these sectors makes organising trade union activity difficult. Figure 4.6 confirms that union density amongst females has traditionally been lower than for males, although the female rate has been higher than the mail rate in recent years.

Figure 4.5: Male and female full-time and part-time employees hourly earnings by percentile, UK

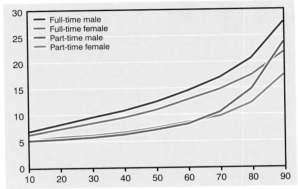

Source: Presentation of the gender pay gap. ONS position paper June 2009, Stephen Hicks and Jennifer Thomas

Figure 4.6: Union density by gender (percentage of males and females who are members of trade unions)

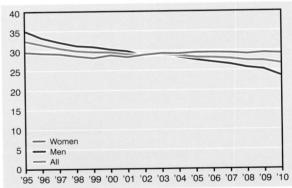

Source: Department for Business, Innovation and Skills – Trade Union Membership 2010 (James Achur) – A National Statistics Publication

Figure 4.7: Female directors of FTSE 100 companies (% of directors)

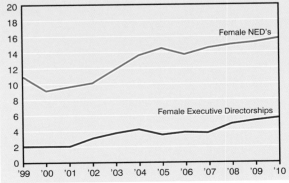

Source: The female FTSE Board Report 2010 Cranfield Institute of Management

▶ The supply of female labour has increased in recent years as more women have chosen to be economically active. Other things being equal an increase in the supply of female labour will lower the female wage rate.

▶ In many cases, females are the second wage earners in their families and may be willing to supply their labour at a lower wage rate.

▶ Discrimination. Academic studies which have attempted to explain the differences in pay by gender have been unable to account for all of the difference in economic terms. In other words, discrimination remains a significant factor.

One particular facet of discrimination is the 'glass ceiling'. This term is used to describe the fact that women have been unable to break through to managerial and executive positions, often because of discrimination. There has been substantial change in this area, however, especially in the early years of the new millennium, as suggested by Figure 4.7.

▶ It is possible that changes in methods of pay bargaining are allowing employers to avoid equal opportunities legislation. Pay is increasingly decided at the level of the individual rather than through collective bargains. According to the Equal Opportunities Commission: "In the UK the fragmentation of payment systems (because of the decline of industry level bargaining, the increase in individual contracts, performance related pay, subcontracting and so on) has led to lack of transparency – employers have more discretion about what to pay individuals."

The special skills that some footballers possess enable them to command enormous amounts of money.

(ii) Why do premiership footballers get paid more than nurses?

Table 4.2 shows the average salary of a premiership footballer over the age of 20 to have been an astronomical £676,000 in 2005-06. In contrast, the clinical grading pay scale for NHS nurses in the UK in 2006-07 ranged from £10,978 to £36,947 per year. Reasons for this differential include:

▶ The marginal revenue productivity of premiership footballers is very high, when gate receipts, merchandising and revenue from the sale of television rights is taken into consideration.

▶ When signing a player a club can be expected to take all associated costs into account. As well as wages this includes transfer fees. European Union legislation which requires freedom of movement for labour has resulted in changes to the transfer system which mean that a transfer fee is not payable when a player moves at the end of his contract. When no transfer fee is to be paid, clubs are in a position to pay higher wages in order to secure the services of a player.

▶ The supply of footballers with the talent to play in the premiership is extremely low and inelastic. When labour supply is inelastic, high levels of demand show themselves in higher wages rather than greater employment, as shown in Figure 4.8.

▶ The monopsonist power of the state in relation to the hiring of nurses helps to depress wages. There are 20 premiership football clubs competing for the services of players, in addition to competition for players from foreign clubs.

▶ The vocational element of nursing leads to nurses being paid less than they otherwise would be (a negative compensating differential). The working conditions of footballers are undeniably attractive and part of the reward for their work, but this has no significant effect in increasing the supply of premiership players and therefore the wage is not depressed by this.

▶ Nurses' unions are reluctant to strike. This lessens their bargaining power. The Professional Footballers Association has rarely had cause to threaten strike action, but their bargaining power would be huge if they did.

▶ The fact that labour is not homogeneous is especially apparent in the market for footballers. The special skills that some players possess enable them to command enormous amounts of money.

Table 4.2: Average salaries of Premiership footballers, 2005-06

By Age		By Position	
17-18	£24,500	Striker	£806,000
19-20	£95,000	Midfielder	£754,000
21-22	£390,000	Defender	£653,000
23-24	£582,500	Goalkeeper	£533,000
25-26	£653,000		
27-28	£899,500		
29-30	£806,000		
31-32	£586,000		
33+	£660,500		

Average for all Premiership footballers

(taking into account only those over the age of 20) = **£676,000**.

This figure typically rises by 60-100% when performance related bonuses are included. Bonuses may include appearance money, signing on fees, win bonuses and rewards based on the team's achievement over a season such as winning trophies or the club's final league position.

Source: *The Independent*/The Professional Footballers Association, April 2006

Figure 4.8: High levels of demand combined with low elasticity of labour supply

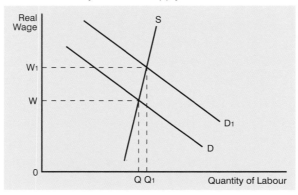

(iii) Why are wages higher in some regions than in others?

This topic is often addressed under the heading of the 'north-south divide'. This is a crude generalisation given that there are affluent parts of the north and poverty stricken areas in the south, but it is certainly true that the average wage is higher in the south than in the north. Particularly stark comparisons exist between the average wages in particular regions. For example, in 2010 average weekly earnings in London were £800.40 while in the North East they were £520.20 according to the Annual Survey of Hours and Earnings. The following points help to explain this:

▶ There is a relative lack of demand for labour in the North East compared to London. This is partly due to the restructuring of the UK economy over the past two decades. Heavy industry and manufacturing which provided a large part of the employment base in the north has been in decline while the flourishing service sector (especially financial services) is centred in London.

▶ The effect of this restructuring is compounded by regional multiplier and accelerator effects. The loss of jobs lessens spending power in a region, further decreasing demand and hitting the profits of local businesses. There is less demand for products and therefore a lower derived demand for labour in the region as well as lower levels of investment. Positive multiplier effects work in the opposite manner in thriving regions.

▶ The labour supply in the North-East tends to have fewer skills which are relevant to the modern restructured economy than the labour force in London. This problem of occupational immobility leads to low marginal revenue productivity.

▶ Potential solutions to the problem including migration of labour to more prosperous areas tend not to occur in practice. This would help, in theory, to reduce wage differentials but factors such as family ties and the expense of moving prevent this.

▶ Where migration of labour does occur it is often the most productive workers in a depressed region who are able to find more lucrative opportunities elsewhere. This is likely to worsen the problem rather than improve it.

Figure 4.9: Hourly pay gaps between white and ethnic minority workers aged 22 and over, UK, 2009-10 (%)

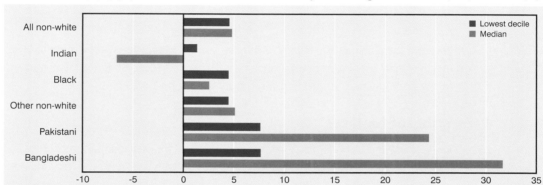

Source: Low Pay Commission, Report on the National Minimum Wage 2011

(iv) Why do some ethnic groups receive lower wages than others?

Figure 4.9 shows median pay for most ethnic minority groups lagging behind pay for white workers. While this camouflages the fact that women from ethnic minority groups receive wages comparable to those of white women, the differential for males is greater than the raw average suggests. Reasons for differentials in this area include:

▶ Workers from minority groups are on average less well qualified, suggesting a lower marginal revenue productivity. Recent immigrants may speak English only as a second language. This reduces productivity and employability, especially in the service sector and higher paid occupations.

▶ As with females, ethnic minority workers are concentrated in low pay sectors of the economy, particularly in manual jobs.

▶ Ethnic minority workers are concentrated in poorer areas of the country, where the state of the local economy lowers the marginal revenue productivity of workers and damages employment prospects.

▶ It is possible that there is a greater reluctance to migrate in search of improved employment opportunities amongst some minority groups. The culture of some groups places greater stress on values of community and the importance of the family than the culture of the white majority. This could serve to make migration less likely.

▶ Discrimination.

The Role of Trade Unions

Trade unions and collective bargaining

A trade union is an organisation of workers who group together to further their interests. The main way in which they are able to do this is through **collective bargaining** with management. This involves the pay for a group of workers being decided through a single negotiation. In some cases, the pay structure of an entire occupation is decided through a single collective bargain, as in nursing and teaching.

The advantage of collective pay bargaining for union members is that they acquire greater market power by acting together. This is in contrast to the position of any worker negotiating individually, who is likely to be weak in relation to the firm, which is often a large organisation.

Collective bargaining with employers may be used by unions to improve other aspects of working life for their members too. These include fringe benefits, working conditions and job security. Unions also attempt to influence government policy in ways which benefit their members.

Partnership of conflict?

The relationship between trade unions and firms can be viewed in different ways. One view is that the interests of the workers that unions represent conflict with the interests of the firm. From this perspective, higher wages for workers mean higher costs and lower profits for the firm. Union activity might then be seen as damaging both for the firm and the economy, acting to reduce aggregate supply.

However, firms and unions can also be seen as being in partnership. This view sees the success of the firm as being in the interests of both parties. A profitable firm is more likely to generate jobs and pay its workers well, for example. Meanwhile, if workers receive higher wages and better working conditions, their morale may improve. This could lead to an increase in their productivity, thus benefiting the firm. In some cases, unions are able to reach productivity deals with employers, in which pay increases are linked to improvements in productivity.

Effect of entry of a union into a previously competitive labour market

For the sake of simplicity it is common to assume a '**closed shop**' agreement whereby all employees must be members of the same union. The union then becomes a monopoly supplier of labour. Closed shop agreements are now outlawed but the analysis remains relevant to the extent that unions are still able to exercise some power over the supply of labour.

Figure 5.1: The impact of a trade union on the labour market

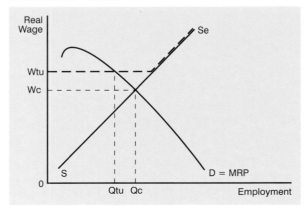

When a closed shop agreement is in operation, the union will refuse to supply labour at a wage below its target level, Wtu. This produces a kink in the effective labour supply curve, WtuSe (see Figure 5.1). The consequence is that the wage rises and employment falls to Wtu; Qtu as compared to a competitive market (Wc; Qc). The market no longer clears and an excess supply of labour (unemployment) is able to persist, even in the long run.

These conclusions are not necessarily valid, however, if the demand side of the labour

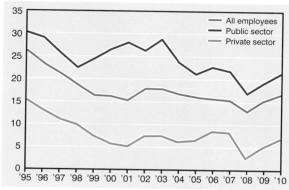

Figure 5.2: Average union wage mark-up for UK employees, %

Source: Department for Business, Innovation and Skills – Trade Union Membership 2010 (James Achur) – A National Statistics Publication

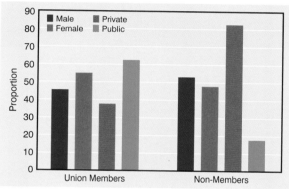

Figure 5.3 Characteristics of union members compared with non-union members, 2010, %

Source: Department for Business, Innovation and Skills – Trade Union Membership 2010 (James Achur) – A National Statistics Publication

market is not competitive. This is the case of monopsony, discussed more fully in Unit 6. Monopsonists are sole buyers of a particular type of labour and can use their power to drive down wages. Levels of employment also fall. Union power can act as a countering influence, resulting in higher wages and levels of employment than if the union was not present.

It is clear that the greater its control over the supply of labour, the greater the power of the union will be. The threat to withhold labour supply can be used as a weapon to punish employers that fail to meet union demands. An important factor here is **union density**, which refers to the percentage of the workforce that is unionised. Union density can be measured for membership of a particular union or for membership of unions in general. Further, density can be measured at a particular workplace, for a given industry or the whole workforce. Higher levels of union density give unions greater control over the supply of labour.

A measure of the success of unions in achieving higher wages for their members is the **union mark-up**. This is the percentage by which the wages of unions members exceed those of non-union workers doing the same or comparable work. Figure 5.2 shows that union mark-ups have fallen since 1995, but have risen between 2008 and 2010, and are in excess of 20% in the public sector of the economy. Unsurprisingly, union membership is strongest in the public sector of the economy, (see Figure 5.3), where there is often a single national pay structure set by collective bargaining between the unions and the government.

Union membership and government policy towards unions in the UK

Union membership in the UK peaked in the late 1970s, when over 13 million UK workers were members of unions, as shown by Figure 5.4. Fewer than 8 million workers were union members in 2010. Associated with the decline in membership has been a fall in the percentage of work places where there is union activity ('union presence') and also in union density, as shown by Figure 5.5.

Factors explaining the decline in union membership include:

▶ Government policy. Reducing trade union power was one of the key **supply-side policies** of the Conservative government of 1979-1997. Trade unions were viewed as a major obstacle to **labour flexibility** over wages and working conditions. Policy initiatives to decrease the power of trade unions included:

- Making secondary picketing illegal. This is the practice of outsiders helping on a picket line. Workers can now only picket at their own place of work.

- Requiring secret ballots of workers before lawful strike action could begin.

- Making closed shop agreements, by which all employees in an industry must be members of the same union, illegal.

There has recently been an increased tendency for strike action in the public sector, for example amongst teachers' unions.

Figure 5.4: Union membership in the UK, 1892-2010, millions

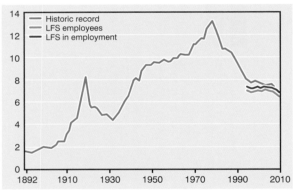

Source: Department for Business, Innovation and Skills – Trade Union Membership 2010 (James Achur) – A National Statistics Publication

Figure 5.5: Union presence and density in the UK, %

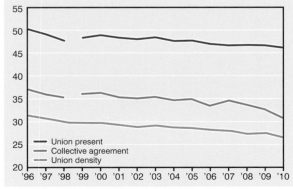

Source: Department for Business, Innovation and Skills – Trade Union Membership 2010 (James Achur) – A National Statistics Publication

Although policy was more 'union friendly' under the Labour government of 1997 to 2010 (for example, firms were forced to recognise unions – in other words, bargain with them – in work places where more than 40% of the workers voted in favour of this) union membership failed to recover.

▶ The restructuring of the economy. This has seen the decline of heavy industry and manufacturing, where unions were strong, and replacement by the service sector. Labour tends to be more dispersed in the service sector, with fewer concentrations of employees working for the same company and in the same place. This can make union activity more difficult to organise. The increasing prevalence of part-time work is also likely to lead to a decline in union activity. Union density tends to be much lower amongst part-time workers than full-time.

▶ Increasing product market pressures. Needing to remain competitive in an environment in which consumers appear increasingly price sensitive, firms have had to strive hard to keep costs down and may thus be less likely to give in to union demands.

Industrial disputes in the UK

Figure 5.6: Working days lost to industrial action, 1975-2009, (000s)

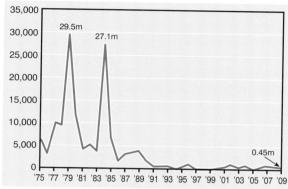

Source: John Forth, NIESP, using ONS Time-Series Databank

Declining union membership in the UK has been coupled with significant reductions in industrial action such as strikes, as indicated by Figure 5.6. This reduction should not be solely attributed to declining union membership, however. Other factors might include a change in approach from unions, such that they attempt to achieve their aims in other ways besides strike action. This may be consistent with the 'partnership' approach outlined earlier in this unit.

In contrast to the data presented in Figure 5.6, there have been signs recently of an increased tendency towards strike action, especially in the public sector, for example amongst teachers unions. This has been largely as a result of a wish to provide strong opposition to government plans to change the terms of the pension schemes of public sector workers. While unions argue that changes to pension schemes part-way through a worker's career are unfair, the government claim that such changes are essential in order to make pension schemes affordable.

The Case of Monopsony

Monopsony power

A monopsonist employer is the sole employer of a particular type of labour. In the UK the state comes close to being a monopsonist employer of teachers and healthcare professionals.

Monopsony occurs as a result of lack of competition on the demand side of the market, in the same way that a monopoly is lack of competition on the supply side. Just as a monopolist has power with regard to price setting, so does a monopsonist. A monopsonist employer can use his power to drive down wages in the market.

Students will be aware that monopoly power is a matter of degree. The power of a firm to dictate or to influence prices in its market depends most significantly on its market share. The same is true of a monopsonist employer. The greater the proportion of the employees in a market employed by a particular firm, the greater the power that the firm will have.

Monopsony in a market without trade unions

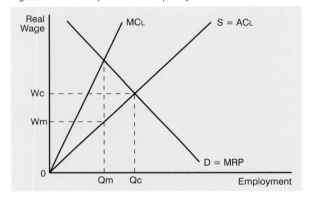

Figure 6.1: The impact of monopsony on the labour market

As a monopsonist, the employer is not a wage-taker. As the industry's sole employer, it is faced by the industry's labour supply curve, which is upward sloping. With its powerful position in the labour market, it can choose any point on the labour supply curve. However, the implication of the upward slope of the labour supply curve is that if the monopsonist wishes to employ an extra worker it will have to offer a higher wage rate. The marginal cost of employing an extra worker (MCL in Figure 6.1) is therefore greater than the average cost of employing labour (ACL) because the increased wage must be paid not just to the extra worker but also to all the other workers in the industry.

Just like an employer operating in a fully competitive labour market, the monopsonist will hire an extra worker so long as that worker adds more to revenue than to costs, that is as long as MRP > MCL. It will cease to hire extra workers when MRP = MCL. This is shown in Figure 6.1, with the result that the monopsonist hires Qm of labour, but pays the lowest possible wage for this quantity, Wm. The outcome in a competitive labour market (Wc; Qc) is also shown. The comparison makes it clear that the result of monopsony power is to lower both wages and employment levels.

It is also evident in the diagram that the monopsonist pays a wage lower than the marginal revenue product of the last worker, in contrast to a competitive labour market where the wage and marginal revenue product are equal. The extent to which wages less than marginal revenue product are paid in the 'real world' is therefore an indicator of the extent of monopsony power.

Trade unions withhold labour if the wage offered is less than the union's target wage.

Monopsony in a market with trade unions

As explained in Unit 5, trade unions withhold labour if the wage offered is less than the union's target wage. Labour supply then becomes perfectly elastic at this point, meaning that even a monopsonist employer effectively becomes a wage-taker. The marginal cost of hiring labour is then constant. There is a limit, however, to how many workers would be willing to supply their labour at the union's chosen wage even if the market were fully competitive. Beyond this point, a higher wage must be paid to stimulate an extension of labour supply. The monopsonist is then again faced with paying this extra wage to all workers and the marginal cost of hiring labour exceeds the average cost. In Figure 6.2, this results in a vertical discontinuity in the curve representing the effective marginal cost of hiring labour.

The mechanics of the monopsonistic labour market are different when a union is present. The monopsonist will still hire labour until the MRP = MC_L, but the wage level (W_{m+tu}) and employment level (Q_{m+tu}) are greater than they would have been without the involvement of a union. You should be able to verify that the closer the union's target wage is to the competitive equilibrium, the higher the level of employment is.

Figure 6.2: Monopsonists and closed shop trade unions in the same market

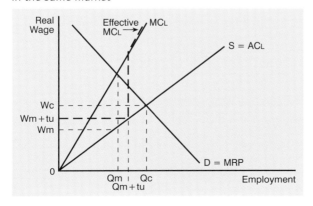

The accusation that union activity destroys jobs is thus not necessarily valid. By acting as a counter to monopsony power it would seem that unions can actually save jobs. Measuring the extent to which monopsony power exists in the real world is then important in assessing the value of trade unions. As explained in the previous section, monopsony power can be measured by the extent to which workers are paid below their marginal revenue product.

Unit 7
Government Intervention in Labour Markets

Justification for intervention

Government intervention in the labour market is most commonly undertaken on the grounds of equity (fairness). In unregulated labour markets pay and working conditions can fall to levels which are considered unacceptable. This is perhaps especially so in the modern labour market where the need of firms to minimise costs through a flexible labour force (see Unit 10) can lead to long and irregular hours, shift work and lack of job security, in addition to low pay. Extremely low levels of pay may be considered a *market failure* in the labour market.

Legislation

The wish to alleviate the problems of workers faced by difficult or unfair working conditions has led to a number of items of legislation. These include legislation on equal pay. As explained in Unit 3, it is now legally enforceable that work of comparable worth should receive equal reward.

Some of the most significant interventions in the UK labour market have been initiated by the European Union. For example, the House of Lords ruled in March 1994 that Britain's system broke EU law with regard to the rights of part-time workers. The result is that part-time workers now qualify for the same job protection and redundancy payments as full-time workers once they have spent two years in the job. Similarly, the EU's Working Time Directive now sets a limit of 48 hours on the time that workers can be forced to work in a week. From October 2011 the Agency Workers Directive entitles temporary workers from agencies to the same basic working conditions as if the employer had hired them directly.

More EU labour market legislation may affect the UK in due course. After election in May 1997 the Labour government signed the EU's Social Charter. This is designed to offer workers protection in a number of specified areas (see Unit 10).

The Labour government of 1997 to 2010 oversaw a significant shift in policy on the regulation of labour markets. The previous Conservative administration tended to oppose regulation on the grounds that it imposed extra costs on businesses and deprived the labour market of its flexibility. Besides the aforementioned incorporation of EU labour market regulations into UK law, the following changes were made as part of the Labour government's **Fairness at Work** programme:

- The introduction of the national minimum wage (see next section).

- A new right to four weeks paid annual leave.

- Paid maternity leave extended to 26 weeks.

- The right to reasonable time-off for family emergencies.

- Three months paternity leave.

- The qualifying period for protection against unfair dismissal has been halved to one year, with a four-fold increase in the amount employees can claim.

- Rights to recognition for trade unions where over 40% of the workforce vote for this.

- A 'Whistleblowing' Act has been introduced to protect from dismissal or victimisation employees who responsibly raise concerns about criminal offences at work.

The impact of legislation

Labour market legislation tends to be unpopular with firms. This is because it is perceived to add to their costs, thus limiting their competitiveness especially in relation to firms from countries whose labour market regulation is not as strict. The notion of a trade-off between equity and efficiency is relevant.

However, it is possible to argue that workers who are granted better working conditions may be more productive. This may limit any increase in average production costs, or even result in average costs being lowered in some cases.

On occasion legislation can back-fire. The two-year rule for part-time workers to acquire the same rights as a full time worker, for example, has resulted in some firms laying off workers before they achieve this length of service. Some firms have been accused of forcing workers to sign away their right to a working week of 48 hours or less. Equal pay legislation and maternity rights may limit the employment opportunities of women.

The minimum wage

On April 1st 1999 the national minimum wage (NMW) was introduced. Table 7.1 shows how the rate payable has changed over time.

Table 7.1: National minimum wage rates since introduction

Adult Rate (for workers aged 22+ until 2010 when this rate applied to those aged 21+)		Development Rate (for workers aged 18-21)		16-17 Year Olds Rate	
1 Apr 1999	£3.60	1 Apr 1999	£3.00	–	–
1 Oct 2000	£3.70	1 Oct 2000	£3.20	–	–
1 Oct 2001	£4.10	1 Oct 2001	£3.50	–	–
1 Oct 2002	£4.20	1 Oct 2002	£3.60	–	–
1 Oct 2003	£4.50	1 Oct 2003	£3.80	–	–
1 Oct 2004	£4.85	1 Oct 2004	£4.10	1 Oct 2004	£3.00
1 Oct 2005	£5.05	1 Oct 2005	£4.25	1 Oct 2005	£3.00
1 Oct 2006	£5.35	1 Oct 2006	£4.45	1 Oct 2006	£3.30
1 Oct 2007	£5.52	1 Oct 2007	£4.60	1 Oct 2007	£3.40
1 Oct 2008	£5.73	1 Oct 2008	£4.77	1 Oct 2008	£3.53
1 Oct 2009	£5.80	1 Oct 2009	£4.83	1 Oct 2009	£3.57
1 Oct 2010	£5.93	1 Oct 2010	£4.92	1 Oct 2010	£3.64
1 Oct 2011	£6.08	1 Oct 2011	£4.98	1 Oct 2011	£3.68

Source: www.lowpay.gov.uk

The NMW is a pay floor (as illustrated by Figure 7.1). The main rationale for the NMW is to achieve a more equitable distribution of income by raising the wages of those on very low pay. It is hoped that levels of poverty are reduced by this. It is also hoped that the NMW helps workers to escape the **unemployment trap** by providing a greater **incentive to work**. Another possible benefit is to reduce male-female pay differentials, given that there is a concentration of female labour in jobs affected by the NMW.

Table 7.2: Minimum wage rates in other countries, 2010

| | In UK £s, using | |
	Exchange rates*	PPPs†
Australia	9.04	6.60
Belgium	6.86	6.07
Canada	5.69	4.99
France	7.44	6.64
Greece	3.47	3.47
Ireland	7.27	5.72
Japan	5.55	3.83
Netherlands	6.86	6.35
New Zealand	5.97	5.19
Portugal	2.30	2.58
Spain	3.07	3.13
United Kingdom	**5.93**	**5.93**
United States	4.65	4.84

*Exchange rates in September 2010   †Purchasing power parity exchange rates
Source: Low Pay Commission, Report on the National Minimum Wage 2011

The case in favour of the National Minimum Wage

The following arguments are sometimes used in favour of the NMW:

▶ The NMW helps to alleviate poverty for those whose pay it increases.

▶ Male-female wage differentials are reduced, as a substantial proportion of those on low pay who benefit from the NMW are female.

▶ The NMW offers a greater incentive to work (see Unit 14 for more on incentives to work). This is of particular benefit to those currently in the 'unemployment trap'. These potential workers choose not to work because the income they could earn is not significantly greater than the benefits they receive when unemployed. The NMW raises the reward from working and thereby reduces **voluntary unemployment**.

▶ As workers escape the unemployment trap they begin to generate taxation revenue for the government. The government also gains from a lower bill for benefit payments.

▶ Workers receive a morale boost due to receiving higher wages. This could lead to workers becoming more productive, leading to an increase in the demand for their labour. This (in conjunction with the following points) then alleviates or even eliminates any negative consequences of the NMW on employment levels (see the case against the NMW).

▶ The NMW should help to reduce the labour turnover of companies. Workers receiving higher wages are less likely to leave to seek employment elsewhere. This reduces the employment costs of companies because they have less need to recruit and train. It also boosts the productivity of workers who gain more experience in the job that they are doing. This serves to increase the demand for labour.

▶ Because firms are paying higher wages to their employees they have an incentive to make them more productive by investing in their **human capital**.

▶ A minimum wage can help to counter the power of a monopsonist employer. In this case the NMW could both increase wages and save jobs. The framework for analysis is the same as that for analysing the impact of a trade union in a monopsonistic labour market (see Unit 6).

▶ The NMW can generate a multiplier effect on consumption, given that the low paid tend to have a high marginal propensity to consume. This may lead to job creation due to a higher derived demand for labour.

The case against the National Minimum Wage

The following arguments are sometimes used against the NMW:

▶ Economic theory suggests that the NMW may lead to a loss of jobs. As a pay floor, the NMW must be set above the equilibrium to have an impact on the market. The NMW raises the marginal cost of employing workers and thereby causes a contraction of labour demand. The higher wage also stimulates an extension of labour supply. The result is an excess supply of labour (see Figure 7.1). Where labour supply and demand are both inelastic (Figure 7.1a) the employment consequences are minimised. If they are both more elastic (Figure 7.1b), more jobs are lost.

▶ Unemployment as a result of the NMW may disproportionately affect young workers whose lack of experience makes them less productive. This is why the NMW for younger workers is lower than for their older counterparts.

▶ The NMW does a poor job of alleviating poverty because it is not well *targeted*. Many of the workers on very low pay are second wage earners in their family and may therefore be supplementing the already more than adequate income of the household.

▶ Many labour market decisions are based not on levels of pay but on pay differentials. Workers not on the NMW may seek higher wages to restore the level of their pay relative to those that are. This is likely to be inflationary and will reduce the real value of the NMW, possibly causing the NMW to be raised and initiating a 'vicious circle'.

▶ The higher costs that the NMW imposes on businesses may be passed on to consumers and may reduce the international competitiveness of UK goods.

▶ Setting a minimum wage at a national level fails to take account of regional differences in the cost of living and differences in local labour market conditions.

▶ A disproportionate number of low paid workers are employed by the state. The NMW may therefore have a negative impact on public sector finances.

Figure 7.1: The possible impact of the NMW on employment

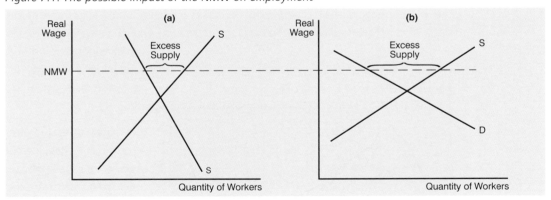

Unemployment and Labour Market Imperfections

The costs of unemployment

Unemployment is an excess supply of labour over the demand for labour. The unemployed are those willing and able to work at prevailing wage rates but who are without a job. Unemployment imposes a number of costs, for example:

- Loss of output. Unemployed labour does not produce an output. Thus when unemployment exists, there is spare capacity in the economy and it operates within its production possibility frontier.

- Fiscal cost to the Exchequer. Those who are unemployed do not contribute revenue in the form of taxation and may be entitled to receive state benefits, such as the Job Seeker's Allowance (JSA).

- Unemployment usually implies a lower material standard of living for the unemployed and their families. Unemployment is a significant cause of poverty.

- There are **external costs** that may be caused by unemployment. For example, statistics suggest a correlation between deprivation and crime rates. Deprivation may be caused by unemployment. Also, the rate of suicide is higher amongst the unemployed than in the population generally.

For these reasons, reducing the level of unemployment is one of the key objectives of government policy. In order to formulate policy to tackle unemployment, it is important to understand its causes. There are a number of different causes, each of which is associated with a different type of unemployment.

Types of unemployment

Unemployment is usually classified according to its causes. With the exception of Keynesian unemployment which is caused by a lack of demand in the macroeconomy, all other types of unemployment can be seen as examples of labour market failure and are micro based.

Keynesian unemployment is also called demand deficient unemployment. It arises as a result of a lack of aggregate demand at the macro level. Recall that labour demand is a demand derived from the demand for products and services. If there is a lack of demand for these, then there is likely to be a lack of demand for labour also. Keynesian unemployment usually arises during a recession and is likely to persist well into the recovery stage of the business cycle. Keynesian unemployment is involuntary in the sense that there is simply not sufficient demand in the economy to generate enough jobs. All other types of unemployment are considered voluntary. Figure 8.1 shows unemployment rising in the early 1990s recession and again in the recession of 2008-09.

Classical unemployment is also called excess real wages unemployment. It occurs when wages are stuck at above equilibrium level, giving rise to an excess supply of labour. Institutional obstacles such as the power of trade unions may prevent wages from falling to market clearing levels. This is the type of unemployment that opponents of the minimum wage fear that it will cause (see Figure 7.1).

Figure 8.1: Unemployment in the UK economy, women 16-59, men 16-64, % of labour force

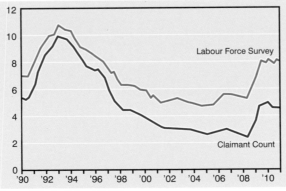

Source: Office for National Statistics

Seasonal unemployment occurs due to fluctuations in the demand for particular types of labour according to the time of year. The tourist industry is particularly prone to seasonal unemployment in winter.

Structural unemployment occurs when the structure of the output in the economy changes leading to a change in the pattern of labour demand, for example where industries close down and the skills used in those industries are no longer needed in the economy. The UK economy experienced restructuring towards the service sector in the 1980s and 90s (see the sub-section entitled *The UK's changing employment pattern* in Unit 2). Structural unemployment can exist even when the labour market is in equilibrium. The supply of labour equals the demand for labour but the characteristics of those seeking employment are not those that firms wish to hire. Structural unemployment is also called mismatch unemployment and is of two main kinds. Regional mismatches can occur where unemployed workers are resident in particular regions of the country and job vacancies exist elsewhere. Skills mismatches are also common, with those seeking work not possessing the necessary skills to fill the jobs available. Mismatches are a sign of **geographical** or **occupational immobility of labour**.

Frictional unemployment can also occur with the labour market in equilibrium. It is sometimes known as **search unemployment** and arises when workers voluntarily leave their job to search for a better one.

Unemployment due to labour market imperfections

All types of unemployment except Keynesian unemployment arise from labour market imperfections. Recall from Units 3 and 4 the characteristics of a perfect labour market, in which no employer or organisation of employees has the power to raise wages above the market equilibrium, perfect geographical and occupational mobility of labour exists, as does perfect knowledge. Now:

▶ Classical unemployment could not exist in this market. It can only exist because an imperfection (such as a trade union or a minimum wage) is removing effective competition in labour supply thus preventing the market reaching equilibrium.

▶ Structural unemployment could not exist in this market. The perfect mobility of labour would prevent mismatches of labour supply and demand. Perfect mobility of labour would also allow the seasonally unemployed to find work in other markets.

▶ Frictional unemployment could not exist in this market. Perfect information would allow workers to know instantly where better job opportunities were available to them.

Labour market imperfections and the natural rate of unemployment

The term natural rate of unemployment refers to the rate of unemployment when the labour market is in equilibrium, with the supply of labour equal to its demand.

It might seem that with supply of labour equal to the demand for labour, there would be no unemployment. This is not so. A glance at the definitions of structural and frictional unemployment given above shows that both can exist even with the labour market in equilibrium. These types of unemployment arise due to the imperfections of **labour immobility** and **lack of information**.

The natural rate of unemployment is of great significance for macroeconomic policy. This is because attempts to drive unemployment lower than the natural rate by increasing aggregate demand will cause labour demand to exceed its supply. This 'tight' labour market is likely to cause acceleration of wage claims and in turn accelerating inflation. The natural rate is thus the lowest level of unemployment compatible with a stable rate of inflation and is also sometimes called the non-accelerating inflation rate of unemployment (NAIRU for short).

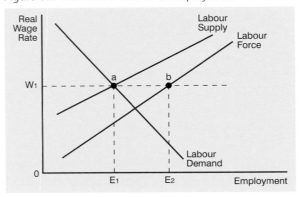

Figure 8.2 The natural rate of unemployment

If all labour market imperfections were eliminated, the natural rate of unemployment would be zero. Unemployment policy in recent years has been largely focussed at the micro level, attempting to remove labour market imperfections.

The natural rate of unemployment is shown in Figure 8.2. The labour market is in equilibrium at point 'a' with a wage rate of W1. The quantity of workers 'ab' are frictionally and structurally unemployed and the natural rate of unemployment is the quantity 'ab' expressed as a percentage of the labour force.

The structure, duration and incidence of unemployment in the UK

Unemployment is disproportionately high amongst some groups within the UK. To break unemployment down into its component parts and examine which sections of society it most affects is to examine its **structure**. Unemployment's structure may be examined by age, region, gender and ethnic group.

Recall that unemployment is an excess supply of labour. Unemployment amongst any specific group thus constitutes an excess supply of labour in that group over the demand for such labour.

Unemployment by age group

It is suggested by Figure 8.3 that the younger the age group, the higher the unemployment rate.

One possible reason for this is that at the age of 16, people have little or no work experience. This results in relatively low marginal revenue productivity and low demand for young workers. As they grow older, workers gain progressively more experience and productivity.

There are two distinct facets of low demand for young workers. One is that younger workers are less likely to be taken on in the first place than older workers with more experience. Another is that younger workers

Younger workers are more likely to lose their jobs in the event that firms need to lay off workers.

Figure 8.3: Unemployment rates by age group, UK (%)

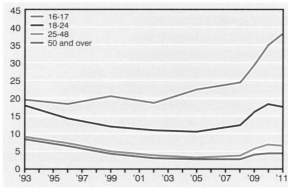

Source: Office for National Statistics, Social Trends 41, 2011 edition

are more likely to lose their jobs in the event that firms need to lay off workers. Firms may be reluctant to lose the services of older workers with higher levels of human capital, much of which may have been acquired through investment and training provided by the firm.

A further reason that young workers may not remain in employment after securing a job is that they may have a higher propensity to quit than older workers. This could be a characteristic of youth, or may be associated with the type of jobs in which young workers are employed. Workers in low paid, routine jobs are generally more likely to quit those jobs than workers in more lucrative, attractive employment.

The supply of labour in different age groups is another important determinant of unemployment rates in those groups. Other things being equal, a higher supply of any particular type of labour will make it more likely to be unemployed. This observation suggests that youth unemployment rates may fall over the next few decades as demographic change (see Unit 11) reduces the supply of young workers.

Figure 8.4: The duration of UK unemployment, millions

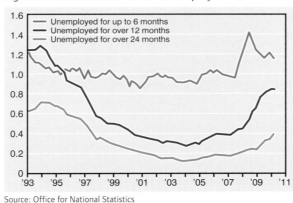

Source: Office for National Statistics

It is worth noting at this point that the duration of the unemployment suffered by young workers tends to be less than that of older workers. Older workers account disproportionately for those who have been unemployed for over 12 months or over 24 months shown in Figure 8.4. Possible reasons for this include that older age groups may be less flexible in being able and/or willing to acquire new skills in order to secure new employment. It is also possible that firms are reluctant to train older workers because they have fewer remaining years left in the workforce. Investments in their human capital may therefore be less productive than similar investments in younger workers.

Unemployment by region

It is apparent from Figure 8.5 that unemployment rates vary significantly from one region of the UK to another. The North East is shown as having an unemployment rate of over 10% in 2010 Quarter 4, compared to a rate of around 6% in the South East.

When a region suffers a very high rate of unemployment it is common for much of that unemployment to be structural unemployment. In other words, there are vacancies available that the unemployed workers could fill, but those vacancies either require skills that the unemployed do not possess or are in other parts of the country.

Traditionally much of the workforce in the North East would have been employed in the secondary sector of the economy, in occupations such as mining, ship-building and manufacturing. The decline of this sector in the economy and the growth of a thriving tertiary (service) sector has not been to the advantage of the area. Workers that had been employed in a particular occupation for all of their working lives may find it hard to acquire new skills or may not have been given the opportunity to do so. Also, the hub of the

Figure 8.5: Unemployment rate by region (Oct-Dec 2010), %

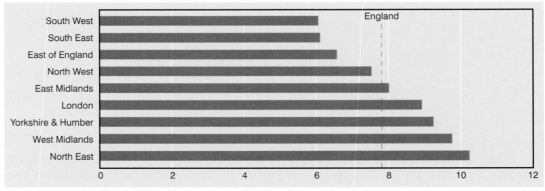

Source: Office for National Statistics (Labour Force Survey, seasonally adjusted)

growing service sector has proven to be the south-east of England. This helps to explain the low unemployment rate here. Much of the South East is prosperous. It includes counties such as Surrey where a significant part of the workforce is employed in lucrative professions, many commuting into London to work in the City, one of the world's great financial centres.

It is possible that dramatic shifts in economic structure which are to the disadvantage of particular areas can set up a downward spiral. The North East would have suffered downwards multiplier effects in the 1980s and 90s, as the loss of jobs and incomes led to lower aggregate demand in the local economy, threatening other jobs. There is also a danger that in an area where incomes are low and unemployment high, educational achievement will be low. This then makes the area a less attractive prospect for firms when making location decisions.

Unemployment by gender
The rate of unemployment for females is generally lower than that for males. This is shown to be the case in Figure 8.6.

Possible reasons for low unemployment rates amongst females include the fact that female labour may be generally more flexible than male labour. Employers are increasingly demanding workers that are willing to be employed on a flexible basis. This may involve part-time work, variable hours, shift work, temporary contracts and so on. Such working practices may make it possible for working mothers to manage both work and family commitments.

A further boon to female employment in recent years has been the restructuring of the economy towards the service sector. There are many jobs in this sector to which employers may feel that female labour is better suited than male labour. Firms may feel that customers are more at ease with female receptionists, for example.

Figure 8.6: Unemployment by gender, UK (%)

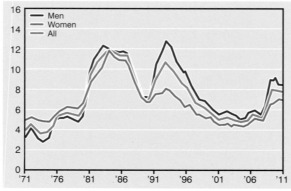

Source: Office for National Statistics, Labour Force Survey

It should also be noted that only those who are actively seeking work are counted as unemployed. Females that are currently economically inactive might only choose to re-enter the labour force when it is clear that employment is available to them. This makes them much less likely to become unemployed.

The definitions which are used in measuring unemployment are less likely to include females than males. The **claimant count method** includes as unemployed all those receiving unemployment benefit, but many women may not be entitled to benefit because their partner is earning. The **Labour Force Survey** attempts to establish a more accurate figure for unemployment by using questionnaires to find out how many people are actively seeking work and unable to attain it. Women may be less likely to report themselves as unemployed in this survey, seeing themselves (even though temporarily) as housewives.

Unemployment by ethnic group

Unemployment rates by ethnic group are shown in Figure 8.7. Unemployment rates for workers from ethnic minority groups tend to be higher than for white workers.

It is possible that demand for ethnic minority labour may be lower because of a lower average level of productivity amongst minority groups. It is true, for example, that the average level of educational achievement is generally lower amongst students from minority groups than for white students. This could reflect factors such as lack of educational opportunity for minority groups. Another factor which may lower productivity is that first-generation immigrants may speak English only as a second language.

Figure 8.7: Unemployment rates by ethnic group, %

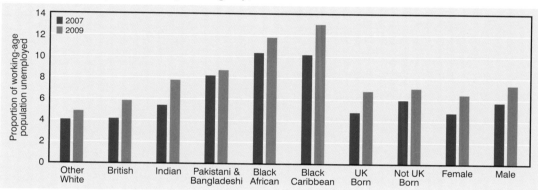

Source: Office for National Statistics, Labour Force Survey

The culture of some minority groups may limit the geographical mobility of workers, making it more difficult for them to secure employment. This would be the case, for example, where the culture stresses the importance of the family. Workers would then be unlikely to move far from the rest of their family in search of employment.

Despite equal opportunities legislation, it remains likely that discrimination against minority groups helps to account for the high rates of unemployment that they suffer.

Government Policies to Influence Productivity and Labour Mobility

Key concepts

Productivity is output per unit of resources used. Thus labour productivity could be measured as output per worker (total output/number of workers) or output per hour worked (total output/number of hours worked). Productivity of resources is a key determinant of aggregate supply in an economy.

Unit labour costs are the labour cost per unit of output (measured as total output/total labour cost). Some data on productivity and unit labour costs is given in Figure 9.1. If labour productivity increases at the same rate as wages, unit labour costs are unchanged. The upward pressure on costs of a 2% wage increase would be cancelled out by a 2% increase in productivity, for example. If wages increase faster than productivity, unit labour costs will rise, causing aggregate supply to fall. It is often helpful to adjust for inflation to find **real unit labour costs**, as in the following example:

> **Suppose:**
> Wage inflation = 4.5%
> Productivity increase = 2.5%
> Inflation = 2%
>
> **Then:**
> Unit labour costs increase by 2% (4.5% − 2.5%)
> **Real** unit labour costs are unchanged (4.5% − 2.5% − 2% = zero)

Labour mobility refers to the ability of labour to move from one sector of the labour market to another. This may mean changing occupation (occupational mobility) or moving to work in another area (geographical mobility). A lack of labour mobility is the cause of structural unemployment, where mismatches occur and workers are unable or unwilling to fill the existing vacancies.

The above concepts are all closely related to the concept of skills. Other things being equal, the higher the skill level of the labour force, the greater productivity will be. Increases in productivity serve to lower unit labour costs. Occupational labour mobility can be improved if workers are able to acquire new skills, while areas of the economy such as the South East would be less likely to suffer skills shortages if labour mobility improved.

Figure 9.1: UK productivity increases and change in unit wage costs (%)

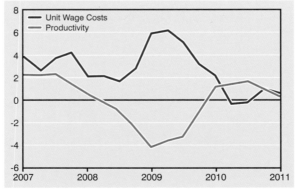

Source: Office for National Statistics

The problems associated with lack of labour mobility and skills shortages

There are a number of problems which are associated with, or caused by, lack of labour mobility and skills shortages.

At the microeconomic level these include:

▶ The effect on living standards of those with low skill levels. Those with low skill levels are likely to receive correspondingly low wages, given that they are likely to have lower marginal revenue productivity than workers with higher skill levels. Low skill levels also render workers more vulnerable to unemployment. The labour market position of those with low levels of skill has deteriorated in recent years as jobs have, on average, come to require higher skill levels. This is a trend which is likely to continue.

▶ A limitation on the ability of firms to achieve their objectives. Inability to recruit skilled labour in sufficient quantities is likely to limit the profitability of firms and may prevent them achieving other objectives such as the development of new products or diversification into new markets.

Macroeconomic effects include:

▶ The effect on unemployment. You will recall that labour immobility is the root cause of structural unemployment.

▶ The effect on inflation. Skills shortages place a limitation on the capacity of the economy to produce goods and services. When aggregate demand is sufficiently high, this is likely to generate inflation. Note also the concept of the non-accelerating inflation rate of unemployment (NAIRU) discussed in the previous unit. This suggests that when the labour market is in equilibrium, with only structural and frictional unemployment remaining, higher levels of aggregate demand and hence demand for labour will cause the bidding up of wages and the acceleration of inflation.

▶ The impact on the current account of the balance of payments. Skills shortages may prevent UK products competing successfully in international markets. This relates to both price and non-price aspects of competitiveness. If skills shortages lead to domestic inflation this will affect the price of UK products which are exported. Further, lack of skills may limit innovation on the part of UK companies and/or make it difficult for them to maintain sufficient quality of output.

▶ A limitation on the competitiveness of the UK economy. The term competitiveness refers to "the ability of a nation to generate proportionately more wealth than its competitors". This has many aspects. The damaging impact of skills shortages on unemployment, inflation and the balance of payments are all signs of a lack of competitiveness. Other ways in which skills shortages could affect competitiveness include that multinational corporations may be less likely to locate and invest in an economy with low skill levels.

▶ Inequality. In an economy experiencing skills shortages there is a premium on the services of those workers with high skill levels. These workers then command high wages, while those workers with low skill levels are left behind. The gap between high and low income earners then becomes greater.

Types of skills

In discussing issues associated with skills shortages, the following categorisation of skills can be a useful aid to understanding:

▶ **Basic skills.** This term usually refers to literacy and numeracy.

▶ **Key skills.** These are skills of communication, application of number, problem solving, team working, information technology and improving own learning and performance.

▶ **Generic skills.** This category includes the key skills but also covers more complex reasoning and management skills and personal values such as motivation, discipline, judgement, leadership and initiative.

Basic, key and generic skills are all **transferable** from one occupation to another. They are therefore an important aid to labour mobility.

Other types of skills are **vocational**. These are technical skills which are specific to a particular occupation or group of occupations.

UK skills levels

Figure 9.2: Productivity comparisons, 2010

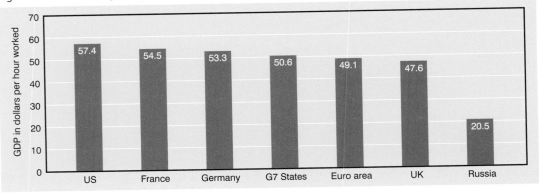

Source: OECD

UK labour productivity lags behind that of key comparator nations as shown in Figure 9.2. One possible reason for the UK's low labour productivity is a lack of skills (human capital). Other possible explanations include relatively low levels of investment in physical capital and the need for improved management and organisation. The UK government has commissioned a wide-ranging review of the country's skill levels, led by Lord Leitch. In an interim report published in December 2005 it concluded that the UK's skills base is "not world class" and drew particular attention to the following points:

▶ The proportion of adults within the UK without a basic school-leaving qualification is double that of Canada and Germany;

▶ Over five million people of working age in the UK have no qualification at all;

▶ One in six adults do not have the literacy skills expected of an 11 year old. Almost half do not have these levels of functional numeracy.

The position in higher level skills is better, with over a quarter of adults in the UK possessing a degree level qualification, but other countries such as the USA, Japan and Canada are still in a superior position. Figure 9.3 compares the qualification profile of the UK population of working age to that of other nations.

Figure 9.3: Qualification profile comparisons

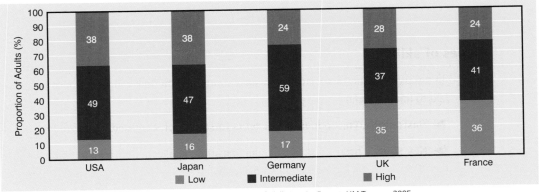

Source: OECD Education at a glance 2005, reproduced in Leitch Review of Skills Interim Report, HM Treasury 2005

Immigration of skilled labour

Skills shortages remain an ongoing problem for the UK, although these may not be as acute during a recession as they are at other times. Since 2001, the government has published a list of occupations with skill shortages. One area of particular shortage in 2008 was IT professionals.

Immigration can be used to fill some skills gaps. In 2008, the UK introduced a 'points-based system' for immigration of workers from outside of the EU. More highly skilled workers are more likely to gain admission, particularly if they work in an occupation where there is a skills shortage.

There are five tiers of worker in the new points system, in descending order of priority for admission to the UK. Within each sector, points are awarded to the potential immigrant on the basis of his skills, experience, and age and whether he will help to fill a skills shortage. Those who accumulate most points have the highest chance of gaining entry to the UK.

The UK points system for immigration

Tier 1 – highly skilled, e.g. scientists or entrepreneurs;

Tier 2 – skilled workers with a job offer, e.g. nurses, teachers, engineers;

Tier 3 – low skilled workers filling specific temporary labour shortages, e.g. construction workers for a particular project;

Tier 4 – students; and

Tier 5 – youth mobility and temporary workers, e.g. working holiday makers or musicians coming to play a concert.

Figure 9.4: The jobs most undertaken by migrant workers from Eastern Europe

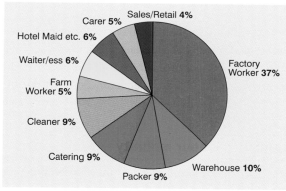

Source: Home Office

Workers from within the European Union are free to come to the UK to live and work. In recent years, immigration from Eastern Europe has been especially useful in helping to reduce skills shortages in the UK. Figure 9.4 offers further details. There is mounting evidence that many immigrants from Eastern Europe are returning to their homelands, however.

There is a legitimate concern, whether skilled migrants come to the UK from the EU or from outside, that a 'brain drain' does damage to the economies of their homelands. Some areas of Poland lost 10% of their doctors between 2004 and 2006, for example.

Government policy to enhance skill levels

One method of attempting to enhance skill levels is to increase the funding available for education and training. Education and training can be considered merit goods that would be under-provided in a free market. They are associated with positive externalities. For example, it is not simply the individual concerned and his employer who benefit from training that the firm might provide for its workers. There are benefits to third parties too, such as the benefits to society of increased tax revenue for the government as the worker becomes more productive, and the benefit to other firms who might later employ the same worker. All of this provides reason for the government to help finance education and training. Increases in funding for state education and subsidising of training provided by private firms are both options that might improve skill levels.

The structure of the UK housing market is likely to remain a significant barrier to geographical labour mobility.

There may also be low cost ways to encourage the private sector to increase the resources devoted to training. For example, the 'Investors in People' award is available to companies proving that they meet sufficient standards in providing for the career progression of their workers. The award may be useful to companies both in recruitment of new workers and in marketing.

Other options include reforming the way that education and training is delivered. The sixth form syllabus is broader than it once was because students now typically follow four subjects at AS-level in the first year of their course. Alternatives to academic exams have been introduced to try to meet the UK's skills needs. These include vocational A-levels offering training in particular occupations and the introduction of a new diploma focused on practical skills, with the syllabus developed in partnership with employers.

Other government policies to enhance labour mobility

▶ The New Deal. In April 1998 the government introduced nationally its new deal programme for people between the ages of 18 and 24. The aim was to help those in this group who had been unemployed for six months or longer to move from welfare into work and to improve their long term employability. Participants receive intensive advice, counselling and guidance to help them find employment or can choose from four options:

1. Subsidised employment
2. Full time education and training
3. Voluntary work
4. Working for the government's environmental task force.

Failure to accept one of these options or paid employment if it is offered can result in the withdrawal of part of the Job Seeker's Allowance (formerly Unemployment Benefit).

The New Deal has come effectively to be a government brand name and New Deal programmes along similar lines have been launched for long term unemployed people over the age of 25, disabled people and lone parents.

The scheme is based on the fact that human capital levels and employability tend to dwindle during unemployment, especially when that unemployment is long term. The New Deal offers the opportunity either to build human capital through education and training or to do so while maintaining the discipline of work in the voluntary sector or on a subsidised basis. This recognises long term unemployment as a waste of labour resources and as a potential source of inequity (unfairness) in society.

The New Deal has been successful in helping some participants to find durable employment, although some have argued that the money ploughed in to the New Deal would have been more effective if used for other employment creation measures.

▶ Policy to enhance geographical labour mobility. The barriers to geographical labour mobility which can best be tackled through policy measures are lack of information about vacancies elsewhere in the country and the difficulty in finding suitable and affordable housing in areas where vacancies are available.

In the UK, the Employment Service is responsible for providing help with job search. An important part of this service is to provide information about vacancies. Vacancies advertised by the Employment Service in Jobcentres have usually been local vacancies, but a recent technological innovation is the installation of Jobpoints, which enable searches of vacancies nationwide.

The structure of the housing market is likely to remain a significant barrier to geographical labour mobility. This is in part a reflection of the trend towards owner-occupation in recent years. Those who own their own houses are less in a position to move than those who rent. A lack of affordable rented accommodation is a major problem for geographical labour mobility. An example of policy in this area is that in the 2001 Budget a 'rent a room' scheme was announced, whereby those who rent out a room in their own home do not pay tax on up to £6,000 of income earned from doing so. Other possible policies would include the provision of subsidised rented accommodation by local councils and help with relocation expenses for those who move to secure work. The housing market boom in the first few years of the new millennium caused increasing concern that key workers may be priced out of areas such as the South East. This resulted in the Key Workers Living Scheme, providing loans at preferential interest rates to doctors, nurses and teachers buying homes in areas where property is expensive.

There are some barriers to geographical labour mobility, however, that it might be difficult or even undesirable to tackle. Family, social and cultural ties to a particular area are likely to make people reluctant to move. In the event of movement occurring, the breaking of such ties is likely to represent a cost which must be weighed against the benefit of increased employment.

Unit 10
The Flexibility of UK and EU Labour Markets

The meaning of labour market flexibility

A flexible labour market is broadly one in which the supply of labour is responsive to changes in the demand for labour.

The key aspects of labour market flexibility are:

(i)   Labour mobility. A flexible labour force will possess transferable skills and/or the ability to acquire new skills, so that occupational labour mobility exists. Another aspect of this is the flexibility to perform different functions within the same occupation. Geographical mobility is important too; in a flexible labour force workers will respond to changing regional patterns of employment demand.

(ii) Flexible working patterns such as part-time work, variable hours contracts, shift work and temporary contracts. Such practices allow employers to vary the hours of their workforce and hence levels of output in response to changing market conditions. This increases efficiency and reduces the cost of production. Shift work can allow 24 hour production. This allows economic capital to be employed full-time, making investment more cost effective.

(iii) Wage flexibility. In an efficient labour market, the wage acts as a signal which allocates labour resources to where they are most productive. In the event of a shortage of labour in a particular market, the wage in this market should rise, attracting a greater supply of labour. In markets, with an excess supply of labour, the wage should fall, causing some workers to leave the market. It is thus important that wages should be free to move both upwards and downwards in response to labour market conditions.

At the micro level, a flexible labour market reduces costs of production for firms and prevents shortages of labour acting as a restraint on them. They are then more competitive in domestic and international markets. At the macro level, a flexible labour market allows unemployment to be lowered by reducing excess supply of labour in some sectors of the market. By reducing excess demand in other sectors (e.g. preventing skills shortages), flexibility helps to prevent wage inflation causing price inflation throughout the economy. The non-accelerating inflation rate of unemployment (NAIRU – see Unit 8) is lowered. In short, a flexible labour market is efficient.

Labour market flexibility and government policy since 1979

Increasing labour market flexibility was a key policy theme under the Conservative governments of 1979-97. This was the rationale behind moves to reduce trade union power and to remove minimum wages, for example. Active encouragement of part-time work and temporary contracts also falls into this category. However, these were seen by some as generating job insecurity and resulting in unpleasant working conditions often rewarded by inadequate pay. For many, labour market flexibility seemed a one-way street that benefited only employers. On the other hand, labour market flexibility offers significant opportunities to some. Many females, for instance, may have been able to take up employment because of the availability of jobs with flexible working patterns. Table 10.1 confirms that a greater proportion of female workers have flexible working patterns than male workers.

The Labour government of 1997 to 2010 continued to regard labour market flexibility as important. Particular attention was paid to the need for the workforce to acquire new skills (see Unit 9). However, concerns that some aspects of labour market flexibility might leave the workforce open to exploitation have led to measures designed to protect employees (see Unit 7). Signing up to the Social Chapter of the

Maastricht Treaty (discussed later in this unit) was an important step in this direction. Some aspects of these measures can be argued to limit labour market flexibility.

Table 10.1: Percentage of employees with flexible working patterns, UK 2009

United Kingdom   **Percentages**

	Men	Women	All Employees
Full-Time Employees			
Flexible working hours	10.9	15.3	12.6
Annualised working hours	4.9	4.9	4.9
Term-time working	1.2	6.7	3.3
Four and a half day week	1.2	0.5	0.9
Nine day fortnight	0.4	0.4	0.4
Any flexible working pattern	19.0	28.1	22.5
Part-Time Employees			
Flexible working hours	8.6	10.3	9.9
Term-time working	3.6	11.6	9.9
Annualised working hours	3.3	4.6	4.3
Job sharing	1.0	2.1	1.9
Any flexible working pattern	18.4	29.6	27.1

Source: Office for National Statistics, Social Trends 40, 2010 edition

Other influences which have led to the development of flexible labour markets

It is not only government policy which has led to the development of flexible labour markets. Other factors include:

▶ Increasingly competitive product markets. In recent years price competition both at home and abroad has become more intense. Amongst the reasons for this are reduced barriers to international trade. Consumers generally seem more sensitive to price than before. Firms have needed to cut costs of production in order to compete on price. Flexible working practices have played an important part in this.

▶ The changed structure of the economy. This has necessitated a reallocation of labour resources (see section on changing patterns of employment in Unit 2). Wage flexibility is necessary so that wages can act as a signal to bring this reallocation about. This has led to firms (often encouraged by the government) adopting decentralised pay bargaining. Rather than wage bargains being struck nationally for an industry they are reached at regional levels, at the level of the firm or even the level of the individual (performance-related pay). This allows the wage signal to function more effectively.

▶ A changed composition of labour demand. This has resulted largely from the changed structure of the economy and has resulted in pressure for labour to be more occupationally and geographically mobile. Similarly, advance of technology has led to a need for the workforce to be flexible in terms of acquiring new skills. Many workers now use computers in their jobs and must therefore possess the skills to operate them. There is also an increased demand for workers with more advanced skills relating to new technology, such as computer programmers.

▶ A changed composition of labour supply. For example, increased participation of females in the labour market has meant that firms may miss out on recruitment of some high quality employees if they do not offer flexible working opportunities.

EU labour market legislation affecting the UK

Perhaps the most significant impact of EU labour market legislation on the UK is that the UK signed the European Union's 'Social Chapter' of the Maastricht Treaty in 1997. This covers rights to:

a) improvements in living and working conditions
b) freedom of movement
c) fair remuneration in employment
d) social protection
e) freedom of association and collective bargaining
f) vocational training
g) equal treatment for men and women
h) information, consultation and worker participation
i) health protection and safety at the work place
j) protection for children and adolescents
k) protection of elderly and disabled persons

Many of these rights are uncontroversial, although others might be taken to be a threat to labour market flexibility by imposing unnecessary costs on employers. This was the reason why the UK at first refused to sign the chapter, leading to accusations that the UK was gaining an unfair competitive advantage over other members of the European Union by refusing to protect its workforce properly. This is sometimes called 'social dumping'. The argument in favour of the social chapter is based on the claim that a fully competitive labour market threatens to lead to exploitation of the workforce and that for the European Union truly to have a single market there must be common standards of labour protection.

The UK has passed much labour market legislation which is in line with the spirit of the Social Chapter. Before the time of signing, for example, it had already been established as a legal principle that work of equal worth should receive equal pay. This can be seen as important in ensuring equal treatment for men and women (and in helping to combat discrimination in labour markets in general). Since signing, the UK has introduced a national minimum wage (see Unit 7) helping to bring about fair remuneration in employment. Legislation on union recognition rights relates to collective bargaining. The Labour government's entire 'fairness at work' programme (see Unit 7) can be seen as bringing the UK more into line with what is sometimes called the 'European Social Model', of which the Social Chapter is perhaps the best available statement.

Specific examples of EU legislation affecting the UK labour market include:

▶ That part-time workers should receive the same rights as full-time workers after two years of employment. This EU legislation was upheld in the UK by the House of Lords in 1994.

▶ The Working Time Directive (1998). Employers can no longer enforce work of more than 48 hours a week. Workers can, however, voluntarily sign away this right. Attempts to stop them from doing so were rejected when the Directive was revised in 2008.

The flexibility of EU Labour Markets

The UK is widely accepted to have the most flexible labour market amongst the 15 member states prior to expansion of the EU in 2004. This is largely because employment rights and protection are greater elsewhere in the European Union, despite recent legislation in this area in the UK. One sign of this difference is perhaps the different number of hours worked per week in member states. Table 10.2 shows the UK to have relatively long working hours.

A lack of labour market flexibility is one reason that most economists do not regard the single currency area of the Eurozone as an optimal currency zone. Economic and Monetary Union (EMU) removes the possibility of exchange rate adjustments helping to alleviate economic imbalances between member states.

How flexible are EU labour markets?

Table 10.2: Average working hours per week, full time employees, EU

Norway	39.2	Sweden	40.9	Cyprus	41.9
Ireland	40.0	France	41.0	Spain	41.9
Luxembourg	40.0	Italy	41.1	Bulgaria	42.0
Denmark	40.2	Romania	41.1	Slovenia	42.5
Finland	40.3	Malta	41.2	Czech Republic	42.7
Hungary	40.8	Latvia	41.3	Poland	42.7
Netherlands	40.8	Slovakia	41.5	United Kingdom	43.0
Belgium	40.9	Portugal	41.6	Greece	43.7
Estonia	40.9	Germany	41.7	Austria	44.0

Source: www.relationshipsfoundation.org July 2011

When countries have different currencies a country which is struggling economically may experience a depreciation of its exchange rate which helps to restore the country's competitiveness. Under EMU, the main source by which a country can restore its competitiveness is by reducing production costs. Flexible labour markets (especially downwards flexibility of wages) are important in this regard. Transfers of labour from member states with unemployment to member states with labour shortages are also important. However, such migration of labour is relatively uncommon. One reason for this is that cultural and linguistic barriers mean that workers are much less likely to move between countries than they are between different regions of the same country. The United States is a good example of a single currency working over a large area. Some estimates have suggested that labour is six times more mobile in the United States than in the European Union.

Professor Otmar Issing (a member of the European Central Bank's executive) wrote in Economic Affairs that the inflexible EU labour market, combined with the high level of unemployment when the single currency was launched, pose an "almost lethal threat to monetary union". Against this background, discussion of ways to increase labour market flexibility in the EU has begun.

The UK's labour market flexibility is one reason for its relatively low unemployment compared to many EU nations. During the 2008-09 recession, for example, the increase in unemployment was limited due to many workers accepting shorter working weeks, helping firms to reduce costs in this way rather than lay off workers altogether. Unemployment rates in selected EU countries are shown in Figure 10.1.

Figure 10.1: Unemployment rates in selected
EU countries, % of labour force, seasonally adjusted

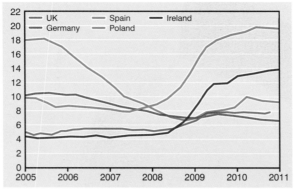

Source: Reuters EcoWin

The need for regional policy as a result of lack of labour market flexibility

One of the consequences of labour market rigidity (lack of flexibility) is that where regions suffer from high levels of unemployment and low living standards, this is likely to be a persistent problem. This is so because 'sticky wages' (where it is difficult, or impossible, to *reduce* wages), prevent the regions restoring their competitiveness. Further, sticky wages combined with lack of labour mobility prevent the reallocation of labour resources needed to reduce unemployment. **Regional policy** is designed to help to overcome imbalances between the economic circumstances of different regions.

Traditionally, regional policy consists of fiscal (financial) aid to affected areas. Government spending provides an injection into the region's circular flow of income designed to create employment and income, these effects being increased in magnitude by regional multiplier and accelerator effects. This policy approach treats the problem as being one of lack of aggregate demand in the region and is essentially a **Keynesian** response that repeats at a regional level the **demand management** policies that can be employed to tackle recessions at a national level.

Modern regional policies reflect the shift in emphasis that has seen **supply-side policy** become more important in economic management than previously. Policies now place more importance on investment spending and private sector activity than before. The rationale for this is that:

▶ investment spending creates new capital that promotes a change in the structure of the local economy resulting in lasting jobs

▶ the private sector is generally held to use economic resources more efficiently than the public sector.

UK regional policy

The change in emphasis discussed in the previous section can be seen in the following elements of UK regional policy:

▶ Enterprise zones. These are areas that are designated by the government for a period of ten years, with a view to attracting private sector investment. Firms can be encouraged to locate in enterprise zones by the removal of certain tax burdens and by relaxing or speeding up the application of statutory or administrative controls such as planning permission. The cost of locating in an enterprise zone is thus reduced relative to locating elsewhere.

▶ Regional Selective Assistance (RSA). As with the traditional approach to regional policy discussed in the preceding section, this involves government spending in the designated assistance areas. However, RSA grants are more discriminatory than the traditional approach in that they are only available for capital investment projects that can be shown to create or safeguard jobs. By requiring a strong link to employment the scheme ensures that the available funds are used efficiently. It is also required that companies receiving grants can demonstrate that the project would not go ahead without the grant. This condition ensures that public sector spending does not merely displace existing private sector spending.

EU regional policy

Significant regional funding is made available through the European Union. This is a recognition that great disparities in income and living standards exist across the European Union and that labour markets alone do not seem capable of adjusting sufficiently to solve the problem.

From the EU's own website, *Europa*, it is observed that: "Major socio-economic disparities exist between some areas of the union. For example, the per capita income of Luxembourg is twice that of Greece. Similarly, Hamburg is Europe's richest region with a per capita income four times that of Alentjo. These regional disparities are prejudicial to the union's cohesion."

The most generous EU regional funding is available to areas that qualify for *Objective 1 status*. To achieve this status, an area must have a per capita GDP which is below 75% of the union's average. Some regions in the EU as constituted before the two most recent enlargements are now above the 75% threshold simply because the EU average GDP has fallen with the addition of the newest member countries. Those regions still need help from the cohesion policy, so they now receive '**phasing out**' support until 2013.

The thrust of EU regional policy is not dissimilar from that of the modern approach to regional policy at domestic level. The financial aid which is given is not simply offered as a stimulating injection into the local economy's circular flow of income but is tied to particular (usually capital) projects which promote structural change, employment creation and higher living standards in the recipient areas. These projects must be specified in a document outlining a coherent programme with specific objectives. This is designed to ensure that the funding is used effectively. Further, the *additionality* principle requires that EU funding should be additional to any existing funding from national governments. *Matched funding* is also required, in that all money provided by the EU must be matched by an equal or greater sum raised from the private sector and public and voluntary sources.

Ageing Populations in Developed Countries

The ageing population (the demographic timebomb)

Demographic projections suggest that over the coming decades the developed world will face a crisis caused by an ageing population. An ageing population has significant implications for the functioning of labour markets.

The problem is caused by the following factors:

▶ In the post war period the birth rate was very high. The generation born in this period are known as the 'baby boomers'.

▶ From 1970 onwards birth rates have been low. This was caused partly by improved contraception methods, including the pill.

▶ Advances in living standards and health care have increased life expectancy.

Taken together, these factors suggest that the proportion of old people in the population will grow over the coming years. The baby boomers are now middle aged and so there is a 'population bulge' in this age range. Over the coming years, this large group will retire but the younger generations are smaller due to the low birth rate. Because birth rates have fallen below **replacement levels** in some countries the problem is not one simply of an ageing population, but also of a shrinking population.

The ageing population is likely to cause problems by impairing labour market flexibility and adversely affecting government finances, especially by making it difficult to fund state pensions. The responsibility for ensuring adequate pension provision is likely to fall more heavily on the individual in future. For some reaching retirement soon it may already be too late to provide for the standard of living they would like to enjoy after finishing work. The younger generation may then be faced with the problem not only of paying into their own pension scheme but attempting to provide support for the older members of their families.

Such problems have come popularly to be known as the **demographic timebomb**. Figure 11.1 shows how the age profile of the UK population is expected to change by 2031.

Figure 11.1: Population by gender and age, 2006 and projections for 2031, UK, millions

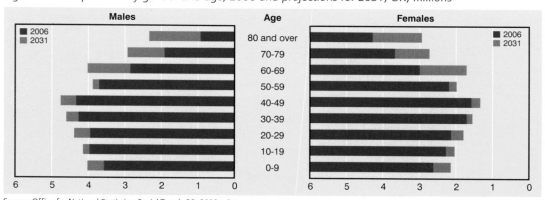

Source: Office for National Statistics, Social Trends 38, 2008 edition

Dependency ratios – measuring the extent of the problem

The dependency ratio is the key statistic for measuring the extent of this problem. It is measured as the number of dependants (those who are economically inactive) as a percentage of the labour force. Figure 11.2 shows dependency ratio forecasts just for pensioners (and excludes other economically inactive groups such as children). All the nations shown are expected to see a significant rise in pensioners relative to the size of their labourforce, the problem being most serious in Japan, Italy and Spain. Each worker must produce enough to support not just himself but also to contribute to supporting the growing population of dependants.

Figure 11.2: Number of people aged 65 and over as % of labour force (aged 15-64), forecasts

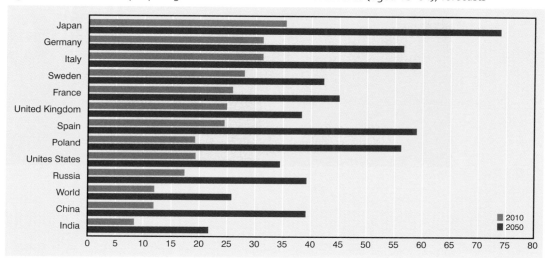

Source: European Commission

The impact upon governments

The demographic timebomb threatens to stretch government finances. This is especially true in two areas in which governments tended to take responsibility in the second half of the twentieth century:

▶ *Pensions.* State pensions are funded by a **pay-as-you-go** system. This means that today's pensions are paid out of contributions made by current workers. This system works well as long as each successive generation is of approximately the same size. A large group of pensioners and a smaller group of current workers, however, means that the sums do not add up. The only way that the real value of the state pension can then be maintained is by imposing very high taxes on those working, which is politically unpopular. The alternative is to reduce pensions. Many feel that this would deprive pensioners of payments that they have earned during their working lives and are entitled to.

▶ *Healthcare.* Over 65s already account for nearly half of NHS spending in the UK. The over 65s are set to increase in number and live longer. Meanwhile modern advances make treatment more effective but also more expensive. NHS care is already effectively rationed by queuing (waiting lists).

When governments provide pensions and health care they are redistributing income. Income, by definition, is equal to output. There is a limit to the output that can be produced by the current labour force and thus a limit to the income which is available to society. Moreover, governments can only redistribute income with the permission of the electorate. The electorate must therefore choose to what extent it is willing for the government to levy taxes, a large proportion of which are redistributed to dependants via pensions, health care and other government services such as education.

Governments have already begun to respond to the problem. In the UK the state pension retirement age is to be raised to 68 by 2050, with the change to be phased in gradually, starting in 2024.

Immigration remains a sensitive political issue.

Further policy initiatives may be needed. These may include measures to achieve better **targeting**. This means concentrating available resources on those who need them most. In this context it implies encouraging or forcing those who are able to do so to take out private pensions and possibly health care. Better targeting is usually achieved by reducing the level of **universal benefits** which are made available to everyone. These are replaced by **means-tested benefits** which are only offered to those whose income is below a given level. Means-tested benefits are criticised by some economists because they provide a disincentive to saving: the worker who saves for his own pension may lose his entitlement to state pension benefits.

The impact upon labour markets

The demographic timebomb implies a reduction in the size of the labour force. Any such constraint on a factor of production, implies a **limitation on economic growth** unless the remaining labour can become dramatically more productive. This reinforces the problem for pension provision discussed in the previous section. Economic growth could help to fund pensions by providing a larger **tax base** from which the government can derive revenue, but, at the very time at which it is most needed, economic growth looks less likely.

A shortage of labour supply is likely to force its price up: wages will be higher. In particular, there will be a wage premium available to young workers who will be in especially short supply. All of this will mean an increase in the share of national income which is taken up by wages and a reduction in the share that is accounted for by profits. The reward to entrepreneurship may thus be reduced.

The problem is that labour supply is likely to be inelastic. Higher wages will not be able to act as a signal that significantly increases labour supply, because of the constraint of the size and age structure of the population. Increases are only possible from the following sources:

▶ Those over the age of 65 (not currently regarded as being of working age). This requires a change of culture on the part both of employers and people over the age of 65. Evidence suggests that there is currently a bias against older workers on the part of employers (despite new legislation to prevent age discrimination introduced in the Autumn of 2006) and it is possible that more people would prefer to retire before the age of 65 than would wish to work longer. In fact, there has been a trend towards early retirement in the UK in recent years. However, there are signs that elsewhere necessary changes are occurring. It is already common for people to work well into 'old age' in the USA, for example.

▶ Those of working age who currently choose not to work (such as students and housewives). Female participation in the labour market has already increased substantially in recent years. There is scope for further increases, but it has been suggested by some that the trend towards more mothers working is damaging to the family.

▶ Immigration. This is a way in which labour shortages have been solved in the past, for example after the Second World War. Indeed it can be argued to be the natural working of the labour market on a global scale. A shortage of labour in a particular national market (e.g. the UK) forces wages up and provides the signal which attracts labour from countries where it is less productive. Despite this, immigration remains a politically sensitive issue on two levels. Firstly, it is not always popular with domestic voters. Secondly, it deprives other nations of their most skilled workers. A case in point is the shortage of doctors in the UK. If this is relieved by attracting doctors from poorer countries it is likely to be severely detrimental to the development of these countries. This problem for developing countries is often called the **brain drain**.

The demographic timebomb will clearly pose many problems in labour markets. One possible benefit, however, is that unemployment is likely to fall. With a shortage of labour it is more likely that those seeking work at prevailing wages will be able to find it.

Another possible effect of demographic change on the labour market is **changing patterns of employment**. This is because as the age structure of the population changes, the pattern of consumption is likely to change to. There may be more demand for healthcare, for example, and more demand for travel and other leisure pursuits which may be popular amongst older sections of the population. This will create more employment in these areas.

Unit 12

The Distribution of Income and Wealth

The distinction between income and wealth

Wealth consists of a stock of assets. The distinguishing features of assets are:

▶ They are capable of generating income. Economists distinguish between physical assets and financial assets. Physical assets include land and machinery which yield services in production, and receive income in the form of factor payments. They also include assets such as houses and cars, which offer services to those who own them. Financial assets include money, bank deposits and stocks and shares which also yield income. The skills possessed by human beings are a third type of asset, often labelled as human capital. Human capital raises the potential of workers to earn income through employment.

▶ They have a market value. The ownership of assets (with the exception of human capital) can be transferred to other individuals. In other words, assets can be sold. The price at which they could be sold enables the measurement of wealth.

Because wealth is a **stock concept** it is measured at a particular moment in time. For example, it is possible to measure a person's wealth on 31 December 2011, but not over the period 2011-2012. The composition of UK wealth is shown in Table 12.1.

Table 12.1: Composition of the net wealth of the UK household sector, 2009

United Kingdom			£ billion at 2009 prices
	2007	**2008**	**2009**
Non-financial assets			
Residential buildings	4,260	3,737	3,827
Other	881	776	796
Financial assets			
Life assurance and pension funds	2,266	1,892	2,192
Securities and shares	666	452	577
Currency and deposits	1,153	1,189	1,184
Other assets	173	197	199
Total assets	**9,399**	**8,243**	**8,776**
Financial liabilities			
Loans secured on dwellings	1,233	1,240	1,235
Other loans	230	230	209
Other liabilities	128	103	87
Total liabilities	**1,591**	**1,573**	**1,531**
Total net wealth	**7,807**	**6,670**	**7,244**

Source: Office for National Statistics, Social Trends 41, 2011 edition

Income, in contrast to wealth, is a **flow concept**. It is generated and received over a given time period. Thus it would not make sense to say that a person's income is £2000, but it would make sense to say that a person's income is £2000 *per month*. An individual's income over a given time period may be derived from the assets that comprise wealth (see above), for example in the form of paid employment or interest, profit and dividends. Income can also be received through state benefits or through gifts.

The presentation of data on the distribution of income and wealth (percentiles, deciles and quintiles)

Data on the distribution of income and wealth is commonly presented by arranging the population in ascending order of income received or wealth owned and then dividing it into groups, such as:

Percentiles. These make divisions in the population at intervals of one percentage point. So, for example, the first percentile of the income distribution contains the bottom one percent of income earners. The hundredth percentile consists of the top one percent of income earners.

Deciles. These make divisions in the population at intervals of ten percentage points. Thus the first decile of the income distribution contains the bottom ten percent of income earners. It is worth noting that it consists of all those in the first ten percentiles. The second decile contains those between the tenth and twentieth percentiles and so on.

Quintiles. These make divisions in the population at intervals of twenty percentage points. The first quintile of the income distribution contains the bottom fifth of income earners, the second quintile the next fifth and so on.

The data on income distribution in Figure 12.1 is presented in quintile groups:

Figure 12.1: Income distribution by quintile, UK 2009-10

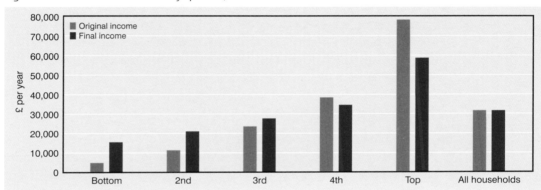

Source: Office for National Statistics

Factors influencing the distribution of income

▶ **Wage differentials.** The majority of income for most people is received as a wage. Thus wage differentials are the most important factor in explaining the distribution of income. (See Unit 4 for more detail on wage differentials) In general, those whose labour is in high demand and limited, inelastic supply tend to enjoy high wages. The opposite is true for those whose labour is in low demand and plentiful supply (see Figure 12.2) Specifically the distribution of income favours:

● The highly qualified. Highly qualified workers are more likely to generate high levels of revenue for their employer (in other words, these workers have a high marginal revenue product). A profit maximising firm will only employ a worker if the revenue he contributes to the firm is greater than the cost of employing him. Thus the marginal revenue product of the worker places an upper limit on the pay that he is able to earn. Workers with high marginal revenue products are in high demand, putting upward pressure on their wages.

● Older workers. This is because the value of workers to their employers increases with experience. More experienced workers are likely to have higher marginal revenue products, so their labour is in high demand. Thus more experienced workers are likely to be paid more and are less likely to suffer unemployment than other workers.

Figure 12.2: Wage differentials can help explain the distribution of income

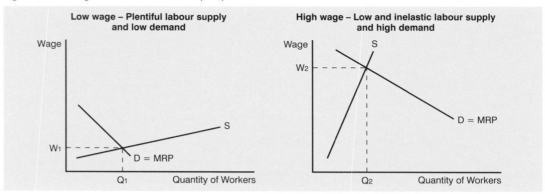

- Those with special skills, such as talented sportsmen and musicians. These skills generate high levels of revenue and hence high demand enables those who possess such skills to command high wages. Such skills also tend to be in limited and inelastic supply, which also puts upward pressure on wages. This also helps to explain the high wages of those who do jobs for which the training period is lengthy, such as doctors.

▶ **Changing patterns of labour demand.** In the previous section it was noted that the distribution of income favours those with high skill levels. This has been more the case than ever in recent decades. One reason for this is technological advance. New technology often requires skilled workers in order to operate it, increasing demand for skilled labour. Equally new technology sometimes results in capital replacing unskilled labour in the production process. Wages of unskilled and low skilled workers have been further depressed by international competition from emerging economies with large populations and hence low labour costs, such as China.

▶ **Ownership of assets.** As explained at the beginning of this chapter, all income is derived from assets. This means that those who own assets whether in physical form (such as property) or financial form (such as shares) enjoy an income from them, thus skewing the distribution of income in their favour. The distribution of income also favours those who own the means of production (capital).

Inherited wealth is perhaps the most important determinant of the distribution of wealth.

▶ **Government policy.** Governments may view very unequal distributions of income as unfair and therefore consider them a market failure. This is likely to result in intervention in order to redistribute income away from high income earners towards lower income earners. This may be achieved, for example, through progressive taxation (where higher income earners pay a greater proportion of their income in tax than those who earn less) and the use of benefits (especially means-tested benefits, which are targeted towards low income earners). For this reason the distribution of disposable income (income after tax and benefits) is usually more equal than the distribution of original income. This is shown in Figure 12.1, where the bottom quintile enjoy a larger percentage of final income than original income.

Factors affecting the distribution of wealth

Wealth is accumulated over time. Those at the top of the income distribution are often at the top of the distribution of wealth too. One reason for this is that income is derived in the first place from the assets that constitute wealth. Another is that those with high incomes are unlikely to spend all of that income. The excess is then saved or invested in other financial or physical assets, adding to the wealth of the individuals concerned.

The distribution of wealth is usually more unequal than the distribution of income, however. Reasons for this include:

▶ Inherited wealth. Vast sums of wealth can be accumulated through generations of a family. Inherited wealth is perhaps the most important determinant of the distribution of wealth. Only a small percentage of the extremely wealthy have accumulated their wealth from scratch during their own lifetimes.

▶ Asset prices increase, on average, faster than incomes. This point refers to the long run trend of asset prices, such as those of housing and shares. The prices of such assets can be volatile (and tend to plummet during recession, for example) but exhibit strong increases over the long term. One reason for this is that demand for assets is often income elastic and rises more than proportionately in response to rising incomes in society over time. This is to the benefit of the wealthy who own substantial assets.

▶ Wealth is less easy to redistribute than income. Governments redistribute income through progressive taxation and the benefit system. While the assets of the wealthy can be taxed (for example, through inheritance tax) it is less easy to create assets for those who do not own them than it is to give income to low income earners. There have been attempts to increase the wealth of poorer sections of society, however. The sale of council houses to their tenants at less than the true market value is an example.

Measurement of Inequality: The Lorenz Curve and the Gini Coefficient

The Lorenz curve

The *Lorenz curve* is a graphical device for illustrating the extent of inequality in a society.

The curve plots the percentage of a nation's income (or, alternatively, wealth) which is enjoyed by the poorest 'x' per cent of the nation's population. It is drawn for values of 'x' between 0 and 100. It might be the case, for example, that the poorest 10% of a nation's population enjoyed only 1% of its income. Accordingly we would plot 10 on the horizontal axis against 1 on the vertical axis. If the poorest 15% of the population enjoyed 1.7% of income, we would plot a point relating to these figures. Note that the poorest 15% of the population include the poorest 10%: the further we go to the right on the horizontal axis, the more of the population is included. We therefore label the horizontal axis as 'cumulative percentage of the population'. By similar reasoning, the vertical axis is 'cumulative percentage of income'.

Two hypothetical Lorenz curves are shown in Figure 13.1. In each case, the diagonal line represents complete equality in the distribution of income: the poorest 10% of the population receive 10% of income, the poorest 50% of the population enjoy 50% of the income and so on. The further the Lorenz curve bows away from the diagonal, the greater the degree of inequality which is depicted. Below, the nation represented in Figure 13.1(b) has a higher degree of inequality than the nation shown in 13.1(a).

Figure 13.1: Lorenz curves

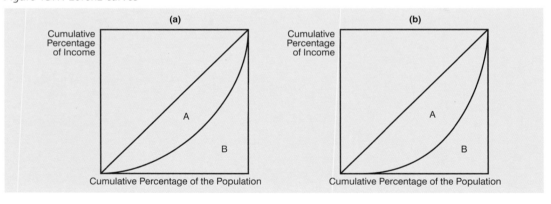

The Lorenz curves shown in Figure 13.2 are based on UK data from 2002-03. Remember that the further the curve bows outwards away from the origin, the greater the degree of inequality which is depicted. On this basis, it should be apparent that:

(i) The distribution of *wealth* in the UK in 2003 was more unequal than the distribution of *income* in 2002/03. It is usually the case that the distribution of wealth is more unequal than the distribution of income.

(ii) Original income was more unequally distributed than disposable income in 2002/03. This is because disposable income is income after payment of direct taxes and receipt of benefits. The UK's **progressive tax system** acts to **redistribute income** to reduce the level of inequality.

Figure 13.2: Distribution of UK income and wealth,
illustrated using Lorenz curves

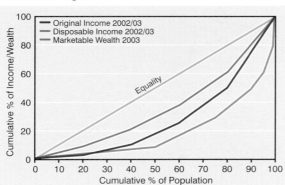

The Gini coefficient

It is now possible to derive a numerical measure of inequality, known as the *Gini coefficient*. The area under the diagonal in both graphs shown in Figure 13.1 has been divided by the Lorenz curve into two sections, A and B. The Gini coefficient is defined as the area between the diagonal and the Lorenz curve divided by the total area under the diagonal or, in terms of Figure 13.1:

$$\text{Gini coefficient} = \frac{\text{Section A}}{\text{Section A} + \text{Section B}}$$

The Gini coefficient can range from zero, indicating complete equality, to one, which represents total inequality (one person enjoying all of the nation's income!). The Gini coefficient can take any value in between and the higher the value, the greater the degree of inequality. This is borne out by again inspecting Figure 13.1. Because the area under the diagonal is the same in both parts (a) and (b), but section A is greater in part (b) than part (a), it follows that the Gini coefficient is greater in Figure 13.1(b) than Figure 13.1(a).

The Gini coefficient is a numerical measure of inequality.

Figure 13.3: The income Gini coefficient, UK, 1979-2009/10

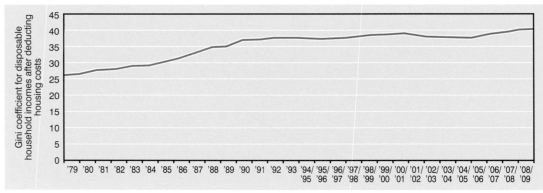

Source: www.poverty.org

It is, of course, possible to quote the Gini coefficient as a percentage figure. For instance, a Gini coefficient of 0.43 is the same as one of 43%.

The graph of the Gini coefficient shown in Figure 13.3 depicts a trend of rising inequality in the UK. The Gini coefficient in 2009-10 is much higher than that 30 years earlier. There are a number of possible explanations, including:

(i) A general trend towards a free market economy, with less government intervention to redistribute income.

(ii) The increasing levels of skill required in the labour market, for example due to technological development. This allows those with skills to command a greater wage differential between themselves and those with lower levels of skill.

Policy Issues associated with Poverty and Inequality

The meaning of poverty

To be in poverty means to be poor. There are two senses in which it is possible to be poor. One can be poor in absolute terms, or one can be poor relative to others in society.

Economists use the term **absolute poverty** to describe the situation of those with income levels so low as to threaten their continued survival. They are likely to be so poor as not to have all their basic human (material) needs met. These needs include food, clothing, warmth and shelter. Some absolute poverty exists in the UK, although not on anything like the scale found in many developing countries.

Relative poverty affects those who are poor relative to others in society. Those in relative poverty might or might not also be in absolute poverty. Relative poverty increases as the distribution of income in a society becomes more unequal.

The issue of relative poverty has attracted increasing attention in the UK in recent years, especially in relation to children. The Labour government of 1997-2010 aimed to end child poverty by 2020, where poverty is defined as living in a household with an income below 60% of the median. This was the position of 2.4 million children in 2004/05.

A term associated with poverty is **social exclusion**. This relates to the idea that the existence of poverty denies opportunities to those that it affects, leading to a variety of problems including poor educational attainment, health problems, high crime rates and so on. The government's Social Exclusion Unit monitors 50 indicators of poverty and social exclusion, with a view to reducing their extent.

Figure 14.1: Relative poverty in the UK

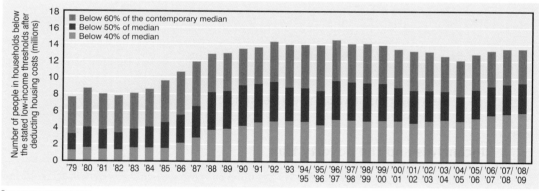

Source: www.poverty.org

The causes of poverty

The factors affecting the distribution of income discussed in Unit 12 are relevant here, but specific causes of poverty include:

► Unemployment
While the benefits received when unemployed may be enough to stave off absolute poverty, they are likely to leave those affected by unemployment well below the median level of income for society. The consequences of unemployment are likely to be especially severe where no member of a household is in paid work and when the unemployment is long-term in nature.

▶ Changing patterns of demand for labour

The 'deindustrialisation' of the UK economy that occurred primarily in the 1980s and 1990s, but continues to some extent today, has been to the disadvantage of many who previously earned a good living in heavy industry (such as mining and ship building) and manufacturing. This is linked to the above point, in that the corresponding decline in demand for traditional skills led to considerable long-term, structural unemployment. However, even those who have been successful in finding employment in other sectors of the economy may only have been able to do so at relatively low wages.

▶ Lack of education and training/qualifications

The qualifications gained through education and training act as a signal to potential employers of the worker's marginal revenue productivity (recall from Unit 2 that firms will only employ workers with a marginal revenue product greater than or equal to their wage). Workers with few qualifications are therefore unlikely to secure anything but low paid employment.

▶ Higher wages for skilled workers

Surveys of employers suggest that many of them are experiencing skills shortages, making it difficult for them to fill some vacancies (see Unit 9). The effect of this is to allow skilled workers to command higher wages, in line with their perceived high marginal revenue productivity. The wages of the skilled workers have thus increased significantly relative to those of the unskilled in recent years, contributing to relative poverty (but not absolute poverty).

▶ Single parenthood

The proportion of parents who are single in the UK is increasing. The incidence of relative poverty amongst single-parent families is high. This is in a large part because the household has only one potential wage earner. Further, single-parents may be unable to work in the absence of affordable child-care. If they do work, payments for child-care may take up a significant proportion of wages earned.

▶ Longer life spans

Life expectancy in developed countries such as the UK is increasing due to factors such as improved diet and healthcare. This means that people are enjoying longer retirements than previously and any pension funds that they built up during their working years must now be stretched over a longer period. If such a fund has to finance a retirement of twenty years rather than ten, it will only yield an annual income of half the amount that it would have done previously.

Incentives and the poverty trap

Policy designed to tackle poverty has often concentrated on the **redistribution of income**. This involves a **progressive tax system** that takes a higher proportion of income in tax from high earners than low earners. Some of the revenue generated from the progressive tax system is then used to provide benefits, helping to alleviate poverty. Benefits can be classified as belonging to one of two categories. **Means-tested benefits** are available only to those with sufficiently low incomes and/or wealth to qualify, whereas **universal benefits** are available to everyone.

The **poverty trap** reduces the incentive for those on low wages to earn extra income. If they do so, they may be entitled to fewer benefits than they were previously. Further, they may lose through taxation some of the income they have earned. The net effect is that despite increased earnings, workers concerned may have only a little more disposable income. In extreme cases, a worker might actually be worse-off as a result of increasing his earnings. The poverty trap affects those currently in paid employment. A related trap is the **unemployment trap**, where the combined effect of loss of benefits and beginning to pay taxation may reduce or remove the incentive to take up work at all.

Benefits can be either means-tested or universal.

The poverty and unemployment traps can be further analysed using the concept of **effective marginal tax rates**. The effective marginal tax rate is the proportion of an extra pound of earned income which is lost through taxation or the withdrawal of benefits. Suppose, for example, that a worker earns an extra £100 of income, but as a result pays £20 in taxes and loses £90 of benefits. The effective marginal tax rate would then be 110%, and the incentive to earn extra income is removed completely.

Clearly, the lower the effective marginal tax rate, the greater the incentive to earn extra income will be.

Also relevant to the unemployment trap is the **replacement ratio**. This refers to the ratio of income when out of work to income when in work. If benefit income when unemployed is sufficiently high, the replacement ratio may be close to one, or even above it. The incentive to work is then significantly reduced or removed completely.

The notion of improving incentives to work lies at the heart of many modern anti-poverty measures. This has been described by the government in the UK as 'making work pay'. Improving incentives is seen as economically sound and is often argued to be justified on the moral ground that rewarding people for work is more ethically sound than rewarding them for inactivity.

Evaluating policy designed to tackle poverty

The main types of measures used to tackle poverty are: means-tested benefits, universal benefits, progressive taxation and minimum wage laws.

▶ Means-tested benefits

Means-tested benefits are a well **targeted** measure, because they are only available to those who most need them. This suggests that they are potentially effective in redistributing income to tackle relative poverty. Targeting measures well is especially important given that government finances are likely to become increasingly stretched over time due to the difficulties posed by an ageing population (see Unit 11). The main problem with means-tested benefits is that they contribute to the poverty and unemployment traps. It may, however, be possible to improve incentives to work by withdrawing means-tested benefits

only gradually as extra income is earned. Some benefits, such as the Working Tax Credit, currently available in the UK, may be tied to working, thus improving incentives further. Other problems with means-tested benefits include that take-up rates may be low amongst those entitled to them. This may be because of lack of knowledge of available benefits, the complexity of the forms which must be filled in to make a claim, or social stigma attached to claiming benefits.

▶ Universal benefits

Universal benefits do not contribute to the poverty and unemployment traps in the same way as means-tested benefits. This is because universal benefits are available to everyone, and are thus not lost by workers when their income increases. The draw-back is that providing benefits for everyone is expensive and thus it is unlikely to be possible to provide generous universal benefits. The measure is not well targeted on alleviating poverty, because universal benefits are available just as much to the multi-millionaire as they are to those who are poor.

▶ Progressive taxation

For low income earners, progressive taxation contributes to the poverty trap, as discussed in the previous section. For top income earners, progressive taxation may also reduce the incentive to work and thus limit an economy's aggregate supply. There is some controversy about this, however. The analysis of the backward-bending labour supply curve (see Unit 1) suggests that reducing the take-home wage by increasing taxes may actually increase the incentive to work for top income earners. Increasing top rate taxes is likely to generate higher revenue for the government. Some of this could then be used to fund other anti-poverty measures.

▶ The minimum wage

By raising the level of pay in the lowest paid jobs some employees may be lifted out of poverty. Further, incentives to work are improved. For a full analysis of the minimum wage, see Unit 7.

Anti-poverty measures

Recent years have seen a radical overhaul of the system of means-tested benefits and tax credits. Overall, much higher levels of support are now available and more emphasis has been placed on tax credits, which are only available to those in work. Specific examples of recent policy measures aimed at alleviating poverty include:

▶ The Working Tax Credit (WTC)

The WTC is available to those on low incomes and effectively reduces the amount of tax they pay. The size of the credit available is gradually reduced as income increases. This gradual reduction is intended to prevent extremely high effective marginal tax rates, which might reduce incentives to work. The WTC replaces earlier systems including that known as family credit. The main differences between the two are that:

(i) WTC is more generous in its size than family credit and more people are entitled to receive it.

(ii) The WTC is received through the tax system, resulting in more money in people's pay packets. Family credit was received as a benefit (a 'hand-out'). It is hoped that the WTC will not carry the stigma that some felt was attached to family credit.

▶ The 'New Deal' for the long term unemployed

The rationale for this policy is that the long term unemployed may be effectively excluded from participation in the labour market if they are viewed by employers as being unemployable. They are then unfairly excluded from the possibility of earning income.

The New Deal scheme is open to all those between the ages of 18 and 24 who have been unemployed and claiming the Job Seekers Allowance (JSA) for more than six months. Failure to accept one of the four options that the scheme offers can lead to withdrawal of part of the JSA (thus giving a strong incentive to work). The four options are subsidised employment, full time education and training, voluntary work or work with the Environmental Task Force.

▶ The minimum wage
See previous section and Unit 7.

Other government policies affecting the distribution of income

Most government economic and social policies have some implication for the distribution of income and wealth. Particular examples include:

▶ The Child Tax Credit
Although a tax credit, this results in a direct payment to the main carer of children. This leads to a small shift in the distribution of income in favour of those with children.

▶ The shift towards indirect taxation
The UK now collects a much higher proportion of its taxation revenue through indirect taxes than it did three decades ago. The main sources of indirect taxation revenue are VAT and specific unit duties. The proportion of taxation revenue collected through direct taxes, including income tax, has correspondingly fallen.

The main economic argument for this change is that it increases the incentive to work. This is because we would expect that taxing an activity would discourage it from being undertaken. To tax income is to tax work and discouraging work is undesirable. On the other hand, indirect taxes tend to discourage consumption. This could be viewed as desirable because it encourages saving, which then provides funds for investment to occur.

The shift towards indirect taxation is sometimes argued to be inequitable from the perspective of the distribution of income. This is because income tax is a progressive tax, whereas indirect taxes are usually **regressive**. Those on low incomes spend a higher proportion of their incomes than those who earn more, because those who earn more are in a better position to save. A much greater proportion of the income of low earners then becomes subject to indirect taxation. The shift towards indirect taxes thus leads to a change in the distribution of income, to the disadvantage of those who were already low earners.

Figure 14.2: Indirect tax revenue as a percentage of total tax receipts

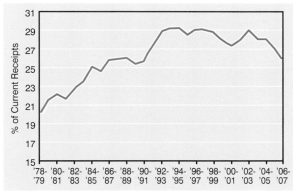

Source: HM Customs and Excise, *Annual Report*, various years

Figure 14.2 shows the rising trend of indirect taxes as a proportion of total tax receipts. Despite this it should be noted that a small fall in this proportion has occurred in recent years. A possible reason for this is that strong economic growth until 2007 has generated higher incomes, which are then subject to direct taxes.

▶ The 50p top tax rate
From April 2010 the top rate of tax was raised to 50%, to be levied on each additional pound of taxable income earned beyond £150,000. This serves to reduce the disposable income of top earners and therefore makes the distribution of income more equal.

Market Structures

When analysing markets, economists usually categorise them as belonging to one of four market structures. In order to analyse the functioning of leisure markets, you will need to be familiar with the basic theory of the firm, which is discussed briefly in this unit. The material included here is essentially a summary of the most important bits of theory. A fuller treatment can be found in any basic A-Level economic textbook or in *Industrial and Business Economics* (Robert Nutter), Anforme.

When studying market structures, economists attempt to analyse the likely outcomes from any given market situation. These outcomes affect the consumer (how much does he consume? what price does he pay?), the firm (how much profit does it make?) and the economy (how efficiently are its scarce resources used?)

A spectrum of market structures

Figure 15.1 gives summary details of the four major market structures. Market structures range from perfectly competitive markets to pure monopolies, where there is only one provider of the product or service in question. In between lies imperfect competition, which comes in two forms, monopolistic competition and oligopoly. Markets become increasingly concentrated from left to right on the spectrum shown in Figure 15.1. A concentrated market is one in which there are fewer firms supplying a larger percentage of the market. An 'x'-firm **concentration ratio** measures the percentage of the market supplied by the largest 'x' firms collectively, where 'x' can take any value.

Perfectly competitive markets probably do not exist in the real world (although some, such as the market for foreign currency, may come close). Pure monopolies are rare, although there are a few (such as the regional monopolies of water companies, for example). Most markets in the real world are therefore monopolistically competitive or oligopolistic. This applies to leisure markets as much as it does other markets in the economy.

Perfect competition and economic efficiency

The features of perfect competition (see Figure 15.1) combine to make all firms in a perfectly competitive market **price-takers**, having to accept the price set by the market. Any firm charging a price higher than the market price suffers the loss of all its customers because there are many firms producing perfect substitutes at a lower price, and consumers have perfect knowledge of this.

The lack of entry barriers ensures that any short run **supernormal profit** (profit in excess of that needed to cover the opportunity cost of all factors of production used) is eroded by new firms entering the market in the long run. This means that in the long run all firms in perfectly competitive markets make **normal profits**. Similarly, the exit of firms from the market will mean that any short run losses cannot persist into the long run.

This adjustment process (see Figure 15.2) is part of the responsiveness of perfectly competitive markets to consumer wishes. In short, when high levels of demand and prices signal consumers want more of the product, then more resources are allocated to making the product (see Q_1 to Q_2). Perfectly competitive markets are said to be allocatively efficient for this reason.

In technical terms, allocative efficiency is achieved where price is equal to marginal cost. This can be shown using Figure 15.3, where the price consumers are willing to pay for a product is taken as a reflection of the utility or benefit they receive from consuming it. Accordingly, the demand curve also shows the marginal

Figure 15.1: A market structure spectrum

Increasing market concentration →

	Perfect Competition	Monopolistic Competition	Oligopoly	Monopoly
Characteristics	• Many buyers, many sellers • Homogeneous products • No entry or exit barriers • Perfect knowledge of market conditions for all market participants	• As perfect competition, except: • Products are slightly differentiated	• A high concentration ratio • Interdependence • Barriers to entry are usually present	• One firm only • Barriers to entry high enough to prevent new entry
Long-Run Equilibrium	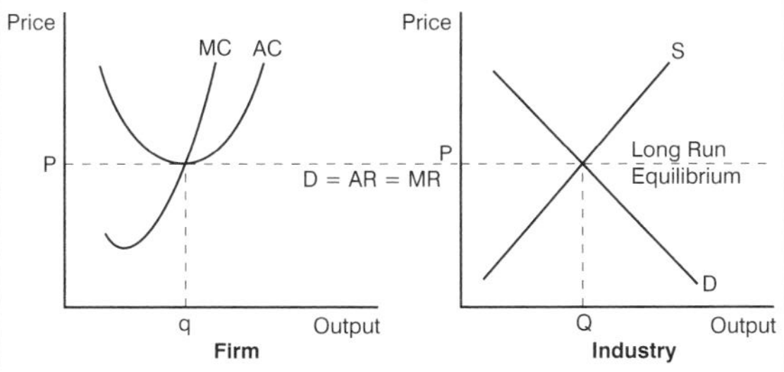	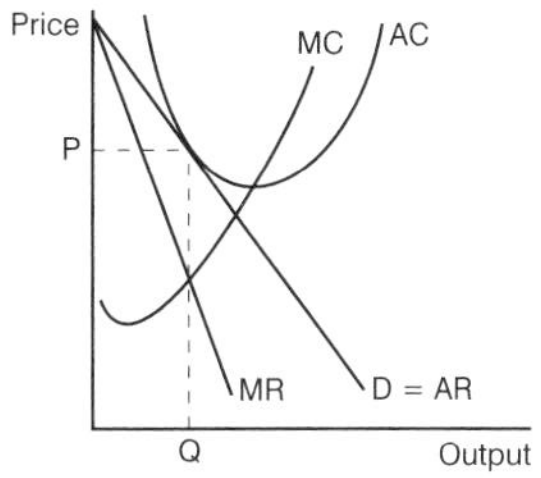	There is no uniquely defined long run equilibrium as such under oligopoly, because of the unpredictability generated by the interaction of the strategies of the firms in the market	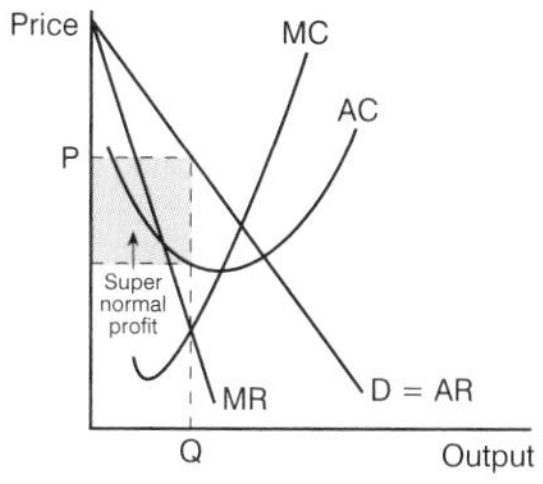
Outcomes	• All firms are price-takers • Normal profit for all firms in long run (but short-run losses or supernormal profit are possible) • Production at minimum AC (productive efficiency) and P = MC (allocative efficiency)	• Firms have some price-making power • Normal profit for all firms in long run (but short-run losses or supernormal profit are possible) • Production not at minimum AC and P does not equal MC	• Outcomes depend on the strategies adopted by firms • Firms may collude or compete on price • Branding and non-price competition are common features	• Price-making powers are used by the firm to restrict quantity and raise price • Long run supernormal profit • A lack of productive efficiency (production not at minimum AC) and lack of allocative efficiency (P does not equal MC)

Figure 15.2: From short run to long run equilibrium under perfect competition

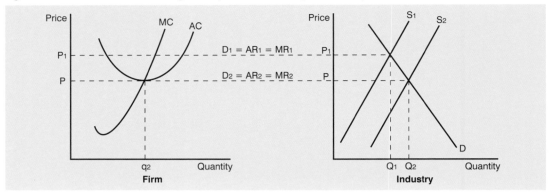

Figure 15.3: Allocative efficiency

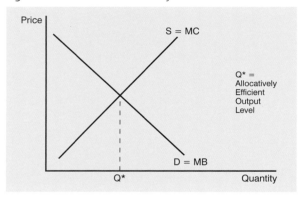

benefit enjoyed from the last unit of the good consumed. The efficient allocation of resources to this market is the quantity required to produce Q* of the good. At any point to the left of Q*, marginal benefit exceeds marginal cost, so that producing an extra unit of the good would lead to a net benefit to society (increasing efficiency). The opposite applies to any point to the right of Q*. At Q*, marginal benefit (which is indicated by the price) equals marginal cost. So it follows that price equal to marginal cost (P = MC) results in allocative efficiency.

Returning to Figure 15.1 or Figure 15.2, it can be seen that the P=MC condition is attained in the long run under perfect competition. Further, production also takes place at lowest possible average cost, with all available economies of scale exploited. This means that **productive efficiency** is also achieved.

Monopoly

For the characteristics of the market structure of monopoly and a diagram to show its long run equilibrium position see Figure 15.1. Note that under monopoly, supernormal profits are enjoyed by the firm even in the long run. This is because of the protection given to the firm by high barriers to entry.

An important feature of monopoly is that the monopolist has the power to raise price by restricting output. The diagram in Figure 15.1 shows that the firm voluntarily foregoes some economies of scale, producing at above minimum average cost (productive inefficiency). It makes sense for the monopolist to do this as long as its revenue increases by more than costs, so that profits increase. As a result of restricting output, price is raised above marginal cost (allocative inefficiency).

A measure of the damage done to society by monopoly is the **deadweight welfare loss** shown in Figure 15.4. This welfare loss is the difference between the lost **consumer surplus** and the **supernormal profit** gained by the monopolist.

Is monopoly power necessarily a bad thing?

Perfect competition and monopoly are at the extremes of the spectrum of market structures. There is some monopoly power for firms under conditions of imperfect competition as well. The more concentrated a market is, and the more differentiated the products of the firms in it, the less likely consumers are to

Figure 15.4: The welfare effects of monopoly compared to perfect competition

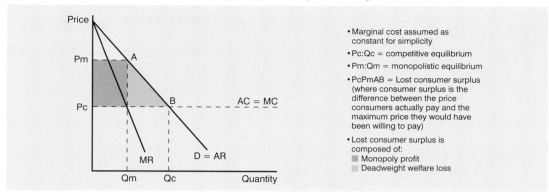

- Marginal cost assumed as constant for simplicity
- Pc:Qc = competitive equilibrium
- Pm:Qm = monopolistic equilibrium
- PcPmAB = Lost consumer surplus (where consumer surplus is the difference between the price consumers actually pay and the maximum price they would have been willing to pay)
- Lost consumer surplus is composed of:
  ▪ Monopoly profit
  ▪ Deadweight welfare loss

substitute to the products of other firms. This makes demand less elastic, giving firms the power to raise prices.

Monopoly power is usually seen as economically damaging, given that the power to restrict output and raise prices can lead to allocative and productive inefficiency (see previous section). However, the following arguments may be used to defend monopoly power:

▶ Supernormal profits may sometimes provide funding for research and development of new products. Against this, the point may be raised that pure monopolies may lack the incentive to innovate because there is no competition. In this regard, oligopoly may offer both the funding and the competitive incentive required.

▶ Pure monopolies avoid wasteful duplication of research.

▶ The differentiated products in concentrated markets offer consumers choice.

▶ Money spent in the pursuit of monopoly power (advertising) may play a socially useful role (e.g. funding ITV or local newspapers; sponsorship of sport or community events).

▶ Some industries may be natural monopolies, where it would not be economically viable for more than one firm to exist. Most natural monopolies are utilities with large infrastructures (gas, electricity, water and so on). The natural monopoly argument has been weakened by government legislation forcing the owners of the infrastructure to allow other firms to use it (in return for payment). Competition is thus possible in most cases.

Price discriminating monopoly

Price discrimination occurs when a firm charges different groups of consumers different prices for the same product, and the cost of supplying different groups does not differ.

In order for price discrimination to work, it is necessary that:

▶ Two or more sub-markets can be identified.

▶ The elasticity of demand in each sub-market is different.

▶ The sub-markets can be kept separate at low cost.

Price discrimination involves charging a higher price to consumers with relatively inelastic demand and a lower price to consumers with relatively elastic demand. A monopoly is thus able to increase its profits. The process is illustrated in Figure 15.5, with the output divided between sub-markets so as to equalise the marginal revenue in each one (failure to do this would mean that higher profits could still be achieved by reallocating output between sub-markets).

Figure 15.5: Price discriminating monopoly

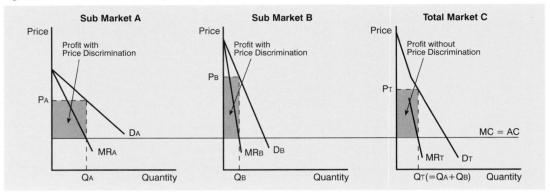

One outcome of price discrimination is reduced consumer surplus. In some cases, however, price discrimination may actually be necessary in order to make the provision of a service commercially viable, this benefiting the consumer. In the case of leisure travel, consumers who are able to do so are given an incentive to travel off-peak.

Monopolistic competition

For characteristics of monopolistic competition, and its long run equilibrium, see Figure 15.1. Firms make only normal profit in the long run. The diagram to show a short run equilibrium with supernormal profit would be the same as the long run equilibrium for *monopoly*, except the demand curve would perhaps be rather more elastic under monopolistic competition, because there are many substitute products available. New entry then erodes any short run supernormal profit, much as it does under perfect competition. The move from short run to long run equilibrium is shown by the demand curve for the product of any one firm shifting to the left until it reaches the long run equilibrium position shown in Figure 15.1

Oligopoly

The characteristics of oligopoly are shown in Figure 15.1. **Interdependence** means that the best strategy for any one firm to follow will depend on the actions of its rivals. As a result of interdependence, the outcome of one oligopolistic market will differ from that of another. However, the following theory is helpful in analysing oligopolies:

Price competition

Price competition under oligopoly is risky, because a price cut may lead rivals to follow suit. It is not uncommon to witness price wars in oligopolies. There is certainly this potential in some leisure markets such as those for air travel and package holidays. A **price war** may be sparked by a firm which thinks it has the potential to keep prices lower than its rivals and for longer (perhaps one with cost advantages, for example).

However, interdependence may also lead to long periods of price stability. One attempt to explain this is the theory of kinked demand shown in Figure 15.6.

Collusion

One way in which firms may attempt to escape the uncertainty caused by interdependence is to collude with other firms in the market to raise prices. This, in effect, involves the firms operating as a **joint monopoly**: they must agree collectively to restrict output in order to raise the price. A collusive agreement may then take the form of each firm agreeing to produce a set quota of output. Informal collusion is also

Figure 15.6: The theory of kinked demand

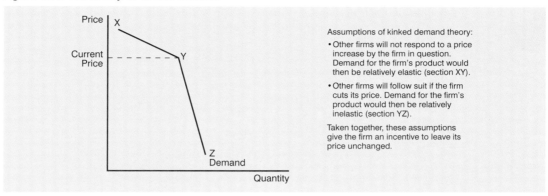

possible, whereby all firms come to charge high prices without any formal agreement, possibly through a process such as price leadership.

Even a collusive agreement does not eliminate the uncertainty of interdependence completely, however. This is because collusion to raise prices is punished by the competition authorities because it raises prices for the consumer. Therefore, a collusive agreement cannot be legally enforced and there is always a chance that other firms may cheat on the agreement by producing more than their quota of output. Any firm cheating on the agreement will gain from the higher prices generated by the restricted output of other firms, providing the other firms do not cheat too. Thus there is a significant chance that the agreement will collapse. Further, the risk of being caught, and the punishment associated, has been increased by recent changes to UK competition law.

Collusive agreements can be analysed using **game theory**. The incentive to cheat is an example of the 'prisoners' dilemma' and it can be shown that cheating is a **dominant strategy** for each firm. This means that regardless of whether rivals stick to the agreement or not, the profits of each individual firm are highest from cheating.

Collusion, in effect, involves firms operating as a joint monopoly.

Can collusion be sustained?

The previous section shows that there is a significant possibility that a collusive agreement between firms may fall apart. There is a better chance of an agreement being sustained if the following conditions prevail:

▶ Cheating can easily be detected by other firms. This will be the case if the output of one firm is known to the others, or the effect of a change in output is immediately obvious in the market price.

▶ Cheating can easily be punished by other firms, for example by refusing to collude in the future.

▶ There are a small number of firms.

▶ Entry barriers are high, so that the raised price does not spark new entry.

▶ Firms have similar costs, so that none has an incentive to start a price war.

▶ Products are fairly homogeneous, so that firms do not have an incentive to charge different prices for their products.

Non-price competition

The products produced by firms in an oligopoly are often heavily branded. Non-price competition is arguably less risky than price competition. Its aim is to win new customers and to increase the loyalty of consumers to a particular brand. Demand for the brand will then be less elastic, giving firms a degree of monopoly power and allowing them to charge a price premium for their product.

Contestable markets

Contestable markets are ones which are open to new competition. They have low entry and exit barriers.

The level of **sunk costs** is particularly important in determining whether a market is contestable. Sunk costs are unrecoverable in the event of leaving the industry and are thus a major barrier both to entry and exit. Sunk costs are usually highest where market entry requires substantial capital investment, although in some cases this barrier may be reduced by the existence of second-hand markets for capital equipment.

Contestable market theory examines the effect of the **threat of new entry** on the behaviour of existing firms. If existing firms have few entry barriers to protect themselves, they may have to adjust their behaviour to avoid attracting new firms into the market. For example, existing firms may have to set lower prices to deter new entry (**entry-limit pricing**). If the market was perfectly contestable, with no barriers to entry or exit at all, this would entail pricing at **normal profit** level. This could result in an economically efficient outcome even if the market was highly concentrated, with little actual competition at present. Note that all of this can occur without new entry actually taking place.

Besides entry-limit pricing, other forms of behaviour which might occur in a contestable market include 'hit and run competition'. This involves firms entering the market for a short period of time, making a profit, and then leaving the market if existing firms begin to respond in an aggressive fashion. Existing firms may act to try to make their market less contestable by building **artificial entry barriers**. This could be done by heavy advertising or investing in spare capacity, to signal to potential new entrants that the existing firms are ready to fight a price war if necessary.

Holidays and Leisure Travel

Holidays

A trend increase in the number of holidays taken

UK residents took just under 40 million holidays abroad in 2009, as shown by the data in Figure 16.1. For a population of around 60 million, this is a substantial figure. There are many millions of holidays on top of this taken by UK residents in their own country.

Figure 16.1: Holidays abroad taken by UK residents (m)

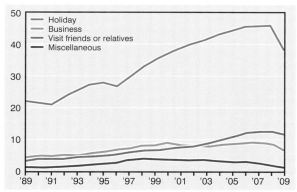

Source: Office for National Statistics, Travel Trends 2009

Figure 16.1 also shows a trend increase in the number of holidays taken abroad. Indeed, the annual figure has approximately doubled in the last 20 years. Perhaps the largest factor behind this increase is the rise in income over time. One would expect that demand for holidays would be income elastic, responding more than proportionately to increases in income. It is noticeable that the graph shows a dip in the number of holidays abroad in the early 1990s, when the economy was in recession and a sharper dip in the deep recession of 2008-09.

There may be cultural factors behind the trend increase in the number of holidays taken, too. Some argue that holidays are now 'luxury necessities' rather than simply a luxury. Britons increasingly seem to feel the need to escape the stresses of working life and while consumers began to cut back on discretionary spending in 2008, many commentators were still arguing that "holidays will be the last thing to go".

Package holidays: Decline halted as 'all-inclusive' holidays boom?

The 'typical' package holiday includes: Charter flight, accommodation, meals and transfers between the destination airport and holiday accommodation. These four elements of a holiday are bundled together and sold to the customer at a single price.

The advantages of package holidays include:

▶ Convenience to consumers, who may find it daunting to book each element of their holiday separately and have to coordinate them, especially when in a foreign country.

▶ Package holidays are affordable in comparison to independent travel. Tour operators book flight and hotel capacity in large volumes, thereby achieving significant economies of scale. Price competition between operators may see a significant part of this saving passed on to the consumer.

▶ Security. Operators providing package deals must be bonded by ATOL (Air Travel Organisers' Licensing). This means that the consumer's money is safe in the event of the company being unable to provide the holiday booked, for example due to financial difficulties.

In the UK, two tour operators dominate the market following mergers in 2007. The TUI group was formed by the merger of Thomson and First Choice, while the Thomas Cook Group was created by the merger of Thomas Cook and My Travel.

Around 16 million package holidays were sold in 2007, a 14 per cent slump in just four years. In the late 1990s, more than 20 million package holidays a year were sold. There are a number of specific reasons for this fall in demand:

▶ Low-cost (budget) airlines have reduced the price to holiday-makers of planning their own holiday and booking flights and accommodation separately.

▶ The internet. It is now relatively easy to piece together a trip using online travel agents such as Expedia, or using the increasing number of websites of airlines, hotels and car rental firms.

▶ Growing numbers of Britons own property abroad, visiting the property regularly in preference to booking package holidays. Over half a million Britons own such a property.

▶ Growing incomes over time help to explain the increasing demand for exotic holiday destinations not catered for by the traditional package holiday.

Figure 16.2: Thomas Cook forecasts for its business

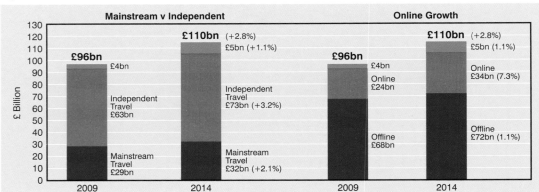

Mainstream travel refers to package holidays, while independent travel refers to passengers putting together their own flight, transfer and accommodation arrangements (also known as 'dynamic packaging')

Source: Thomas Cook Group PLC, Market Report 2010

Since 2008, there have been signs of the market for package holidays stabilising. Indeed, Figure 16.2 shows that Thomas Cook expects its package holiday business to grow modestly by 2.1% between 2010 and 2014. Furthermore, the 'all-inclusive' sector of the package market has been growing rapidly. This has led First Choice to announce that it will sell only all-inclusive holidays from Summer 2012 onwards. Reasons for the stabilisation of demand for package holidays and the growing popularity of all-inclusive holidays include:

▶ The impact of the recession of 2008-09 and the squeeze on real incomes during the recovery. Real household disposable income fell by 0.8% in 2010 (the biggest fall for 30 years) as wages failed to keep pace with prices. This has caused consumers to seek 'value for money' which all-inclusive holidays are perceived to offer.

▶ The weakness of the pound. The effective Sterling exchange rate (the value of Sterling against a trade-weighted basket of other currencies) fell by about 25% between 2007 and 2009. This makes meals and drinks more expensive to buy for Britons travelling to other countries, making all-inclusive holidays more popular.

▶ The collapse of some low budget air lines and some holiday firms (such as Sun4U in 2010) has reminded consumers of the security value of the package holiday (see the point on security earlier in this section).

Tour operators introduce 'dynamic packaging' and move on-line

In response to challenges in the package holiday market, tour operators have adopted a number of approaches. These include:

▶ 'Dynamic packaging' and 'niche marketing' have become important concepts for tour operators. Dynamic packaging allows tourists to put together their own package by choosing each individual component of the package from a range offered by the tour operator. Figure 16.2 indicates that Thomas Cook expects strong growth in this area of its business. Niche marketing provides packages targeted at particular types of customers, such as those requiring adventure holidays, sporting activity or unusual destinations. By their nature, niche holidays do not sell in as large volumes as traditional packages, but they do sell at higher prices and offer higher profit margins per holiday sold. This is because demand for niche holidays is inelastic with respect to price.

▶ Tour operators are moving an increasing amount of their business on-line. Their trusted reputation may provide them with a significant advantage when competing for business on-line against smaller and less well-known firms. Rapid growth of online sales is forecasted by Thomas Cook (see Figure 16.2).

Continuing integration amongst tour operators

The UK now has two giant tour operators co-existing with a number of smaller firms. The two giants have been created through horizontal integration in a series of mergers. This came to a head when the 'big four' became the 'big two' in 2007, with TUI Thomson and First Choice coming together under the TUI Travel banner, and the Thomas Cook group being created by the merger of Thomas Cook and My Travel.

Effects of horizontal integration include:

▶ Economies of scale. The Thomson/First Choice merger was predicted to make cost savings of £100m within three years, with two-thirds of this coming from rationalisation to avoid duplication of administrative structures.

▶ Elimination of competition and acquisition of greater market power. One possible effect of the increased concentration amongst tour operators is higher prices and reduced competition as the market tends towards monopoly. However, this may not happen as the newly merged firms attempt to maintain market share in the face of competition from holiday makers arranging their holidays independently. The mergers were passed by the EU competition authorities who might have vetoed them had they been concerned about monopoly power.

▶ Diversification. The 'big four' had acquired many smaller operators prior to becoming the 'big two'. Many of the firms acquired are operators in niche markets carrying higher profit margins.

The business model of tour operators has traditionally been based on **vertical integration**. For example, Thomson owned its own travel agent in Lunn Poly (forwards vertical integration) and its own airline, Britannia (backwards vertical integration). This offered Thomson the significant advantages of a guaranteed supply of air seats and the opportunity to offer preferential treatment to the sale of its own holidays in Lunn Poly estate agents. Thomson would also enjoy the profits generated by the businesses that it had acquired. The major tour operators still operate on a vertically integrated basis, although the airlines and travel agents that they own may now carry the same brand name as the tour operator.

A further possibility for backwards vertical integration is the acquisition of hotels by tour operators. At present, tour operators have chosen not to pursue this option, judging that hotel management is better performed by those who specialise in the business.

Pricing strategy in the package holiday market

The classic dilemma for firms operating in an oligopolistic market such as that for package holidays is whether to compete on price. The interdependence between the large firms dominating the market is such that competing on price may lead to a price war. If this occurs, profit margins on each product unit sold are reduced for all firms, with their respective market shares being little changed. Pricing decisions in the package holiday market can be thought of in terms of short and long run pricing strategies.

Short run pricing strategy

For any given holiday season, tour operators have a certain number of holidays to sell. This capacity is fixed perhaps 12 months in advance by bookings made with hoteliers and the establishing of flight schedules for the chartered airlines owned by the tour operators. The costs associated with hotel rooms and seats on flights can thus be regarded as **fixed costs** of the tour operator and must be paid even in the event that the package holidays of which they form a part are not sold. In this sense they are also **sunk costs**, which are unrecoverable.

Because such costs are a large proportion of the total costs of a tour operator, it becomes crucial that each operator should use as much of its pre-booked capacity as possible. It can ill-afford to pay for empty hotel rooms and unoccupied seats on aircraft. When the departure date for a holiday is near, and the holiday has not yet been sold, this puts severe pressure on the tour operator to sell the holiday at a discounted price. It will make sense to sell the holiday even at a very low price as long as that price exceeds the minimal variable costs of the holiday (such as in-flight meals and airport taxes).

It can be seen from the above that price competition during the selling period for any given holiday season is virtually inevitable. As long as there are surplus holidays to sell, prices will fall. This is simply the result of the **price mechanism** acting to eliminate excess supply.

It should be noted, however, that the extent of any discounting depends on how much capacity the tour operators have booked in advance of the selling period. Sometimes the operators respond to a season in which they have had to discount holidays heavily by cutting back on capacity for the following year, in which case fewer discounts will be available. Note also that the price of holidays does not always fall as the departure date approaches. If tour operators have discounted a particular holiday to eliminate spare capacity, a rush of bookings for that holiday may lead them to raise the price again as remaining places become scarce.

Long run pricing strategy

If price competition in the short run is a predictable feature of the package holiday market, the more interesting strategic decisions are taken in the long term. In particular, how much capacity should each major tour operator book 12 months or more in advance of the holiday season? This involves forecasting demand and predicting the strategies of competitors – **interdependence** at work. TUI Travel announced in November 2008 that they were reducing capacity by 27% for 2009. Thomas Cook also announced sharp reductions.

International leisure travel

International leisure travel is largely by air

The majority of international leisure travel is undertaken by air. Figure 16.3 shows the number of visits abroad undertaken by UK residents by different modes of travel.

Figure 16.3: UK resident trips abroad by mode of travel

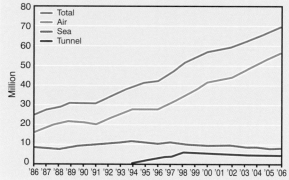

Source: Office for National Statistics, Travel Trends 2006

Although some of the trips accounted for by the data were actually for business purposes, the vast majority were leisure trips, predominantly holidays. The sea or tunnel are popular for some leisure purposes, for example taking a car to mainland Europe.

International leisure travel providers and the recession

As the UK dipped into recession in 2008, it became likely that airlines, tour operators and others involved in the international leisure travel market would face difficult times. A number of businesses, notably budget airlines, failed during the year. Perhaps the most prominent closure was that of XL Leisure in September. XL was the UK's third largest tour operator and a significant player in the budget airline market.

A key reason for these failures was very high oil (and therefore aircraft fuel) prices, hitting $140 per barrel in the summer of 2008. Although oil prices collapsed to less than $50 a barrel by the end of the year, this came too late to save many firms.

Further challenges lay ahead:

▶ Consumers cut discretionary spending during the recession and were more reluctant to undertake international travel.

▶ Unemployment rose. Those who are unemployed are unlikely to travel abroad at all.

▶ By the end of 2008, Sterling had weakened very considerably against major currencies such as the Dollar and the Euro and looked likely to remain so for some time. This raised the costs of tour operators who have to pay for capacity in foreign currencies. It also reduced the power of Britons travelling in foreign countries, making them less likely to choose holidays or other leisure trips abroad.

▶ Rising Air Passenger Duty.

Air travel

Market structure

Figure 16.4 shows the relative sizes of the leading UK airlines, as measured by tonnes of passengers and cargo carried multiplied by kilometres travelled. There are many other ways of measuring the size of airlines but this data suggests an oligopolistic market structure for air travel. British Airways might be argued to be a dominant firm in the market. There is a 5-firm concentration ratio of 74% of all tonne-kilometres used by UK airlines.

Figure 16.4: Percentage of tonne-kilometres used by UK airlines, 2007

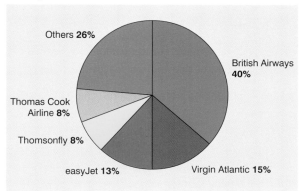

Source: Based on data from UK Airline Statistics 2010 (www.caa.co.uk)

It may be helpful to think of air travel as consisting of distinct markets for each available route. The picture of a concentrated market still applies here as there are likely to be only a small number of airlines serving any one route. Another feature of oligopoly, interdependence, is also relevant. For example, a change in the pricing strategy of any one airline will significantly affect the strategy of other companies serving the same route. Considerable barriers to entry are also present (see following section).

Entry barriers and contestability

Markets for air travel have traditionally been very difficult to enter. A major reason is that markets have been strongly regulated by governments to limit access.

Low cost airlines aim to win customers by charging lower fares.

However, entry barriers have been reduced significantly in recent years. Most important in this regard has been the negotiation of 'open skies' agreements. Under the EU open skies agreement it has been possible since 1997 for any airline based in an EU member state to operate flights between any two points in Europe. In March 2008, an open skies agreement between the EU and the USA came into effect. It would now be possible (subject to availability of take-off and landing slots) for a German airline to offer flights to the USA from London, rather than just from Frankfurt.

The low-cost airline model (see following section) has also made it easier to enter markets for air travel.

Despite these factors, significant entry barriers remain:

▶ The cost of buying or leasing aircraft. This requires substantial initial investment and may be, at least in part, a sunk cost unrecoverable in the event that the firm leaves the industry.

▶ The availability of suitable take-off and landing slots at airports. These are increasingly scarce due to new entry that has already occurred.

▶ Obtaining an air operator's license.

▶ Lack of ability to exploit economies of scale. New entrants may be small, at least initially, and not able to take advantage of the significant economies of scale available in air travel. The large economies of scale available suggest that future trends may be towards the merger of existing airlines rather than market entry by new ones.

▶ Overcoming any brand loyalty enjoyed by companies already serving the routes concerned.

▶ Most busy, highly profitable routes are already served by one or more 'low-cost airlines' competing mainly on price and larger, longer established airlines competing on other factors, such as comfort and quality of service. This may leave little room for substantial new entry.

▶ The possibility of further government intervention to limit air travel for environmental reasons may discourage new entry.

Low-cost airlines

Low cost airlines such as easyJet compete on price, aiming to win customers from longer established airlines by charging lower fares. In order to do this, costs are minimised and only basic service is offered. Examples of ways in which low cost airlines reduce their costs include:

▶ Ticketless travel. No tickets are issued. Nearly all customers book on the internet and need only their booking reference and passport to travel.

▶ No in-flight meals.

▶ Use of cheaper airports such as Luton, rather than more expensive ones such as Heathrow.

▶ Efficient use of airports. Low cost airlines have reduced the turnaround time from planes landing to taking off with new passengers to 30 minutes and below. This means that the fixed costs of aircraft can be spread over a greater number of passengers. Reducing fixed costs is important, because these can amount up to 70% of the cost of an airline.

In 2008 high oil prices led to the collapse of a number of budget airlines, including Zoom, Silverjet and XL. Analysts began to cast doubt on the future of the low-cost model, in the face of higher Air Passenger Duty.

Competition

Oligopolistic markets are often characterised by price rigidity. This is because interdependence makes it possible that any moves to undercut rivals on price will result in a full-blown price war. Price rigidity has certainly not been a feature in air travel over recent years, however. The main reason for this has been the destabilising effect of market entry by low cost airlines, with a strategy of competing on price to win passengers. As a strategy, this has considerable scope for success: as long as passengers are happy to travel with a 'no frills' service, the services of one airline will be a good substitute for any other airline on the same route, and there will be a high **cross-price elasticity of demand** between the services. However, price competition is limited to some extent by the fact that it is rare for two low cost airlines to compete against one another by flying the same route.

Longer established airlines have two possible means of combating the challenge provided by low-cost airlines. One is to cut their own fares. This has undoubtedly occurred and requires established airlines either to accept a lower profit margin on each passenger they carry or to remodel themselves to reduce costs in much the same way as airlines such as easyJet. This approach has been adopted by a number of established airlines. British Airways now runs a low fare service on a number of routes where it is faced by competition from new entrants. British Midland operates in a similar way with its 'BMI baby' service.

The other possible response to new entrants is for established airlines to attempt to reinforce customer loyalty through a range of measures under the heading of non-price competition. These include frequent flyer schemes, and competition on quality of service including meals, in-flight entertainment and comfort (leg room, for example). These measures serve to reduce elasticity of demand, allowing established airlines to sustain price differentials between themselves and new low cost entrants. In some cases, passengers may be willing to pay a very substantial price premium for executive class services.

Integration

The economies of scale available in air travel are huge. This arises because the large fixed costs of air travel can be spread over more customers. **Horizontal integration** offers opportunity for exploiting many of these economies of scale, for example by rationalising to avoid wasteful duplication. It may be possible for the merged company to operate with fewer aircraft than the combined fleet of the two companies previously existing. This is especially the case if the two companies previously competed on the same route. In the case of easyJet and Go, who merged in August 2002, significant savings have been made by merging the booking systems of the two companies. The competitive pressures existing in air travel today, along with the economies of scale available, suggest that future consolidation of the industry through mergers is likely.

Air travel and environmental issues

The environmental impact of air travel is giving governments major cause for concern. Continued growth of air travel and the transport of freight by air is seen as essential to future economic growth facilitated by international trade. On the other hand, air travel contributes significantly to the **negative externality** of global warming. Over the last 30 years the carbon dioxide emissions output by UK air travel have more than trebled to about 38 million tonnes per year. Because aircraft release carbon dioxide high in the atmosphere they have a greater global warming effect than other sources of carbon dioxide emissions.

Governments are coming under increasing pressure from lobbyists to place environmental taxes on air travel, but few governments have been willing to take this move in isolation. This is because it would increase costs of air travel to and from the country concerned, handing a competitive advantage to other nations who did not impose such a tax. However, changes to the UK's Air Passenger Duty announced in November 2008 are designed to make long-haul flying significantly more expensive.

Environmental considerations are also important in evaluating plans for new airports and additional terminals at existing airports. Without additional airport capacity, future growth of air travel will be curtailed. Factors such as increased road traffic in the areas surrounding new terminals, use of green space for building new terminals and noise pollution from aircraft all need to be considered.

Cinema Admissions

The enduring popularity of the cinema

Going to the cinema is an enduringly popular leisure pursuit. It is one of a number of ways of watching films, at the end of the supply chain shown in Figure 17.1.

Other ways of watching film are in many respects good substitutes for trips to the cinema, but survey evidence suggests that the majority of people prefer to watch films at the cinema to watching at home, the 'cinema experience' seen as being more enjoyable. The popularity of the cinema is also boosted by the fact that films are shown at cinemas some months before they are released on DVD or video.

Compared with many alternative ways of spending a night out, the cinema is significantly cheaper. This too helps to explain its continued success. A further factor is that it can also be combined with other leisure activities such as meeting with friends for a drink before or after the film.

Figure 17.1: The supply chain for film

Cinema (£944m)	**TV (£1.1bn)**	**Video on demand (£124m)**	**Film sales**	**Film rentals**
E.g. Odeon, Cineworld, Vue	Terrestrial channels (BBC1 through to Five) or multi-channel (pay or free to air)	From providers such as Virgin, Sky or Top Up TV or from the internet	Mainly in DVD, Blu-ray or video cassette format	Mainly in DVD, Blu-ray or video cassette format

(£1.51bn)

Exhibition of films

Distribution of films

The top five distributors of films in the UK in 2007 were Warner Bros, Paramount, 20th Century Fox, Universal Pictures and Walt Disney studios, with a collective market share of almost 69%.

Production of films

Many films that are successful in the UK are produced in the USA. However, the number and popularity of UK produced films has increased in recent years.

Figures in brackets show the revenue derived from each mode of watching films in 2009, from the UK Film Council Statistical Year Book 2010. With total revenue of £3.7bn, the UK had the third largest filmed entertainment market behind the USA and Japan.

Figure 17.2: UK cinema admissions, millions

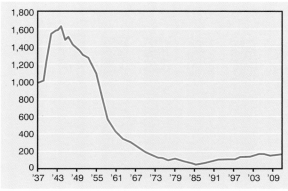

Source: UK Film Council Yearbook 2010

Figure 17.2 shows that UK cinema admissions are a long way short of their peak in the 1940s. However, they have shown a significant trend increase since the mid 1980s

Factors affecting demand for cinema admissions

▶ The price of cinema tickets – Screen Digest suggest that the average price of a ticket at UK cinemas in 2010 was £5.95 (an increase of over 9% from the previous year). One might expect demand for cinema tickets to be price elastic given the alternative ways of watching films. However, as discussed in the previous section, a trip to the cinema seems to be regarded as preferable to substitutes and therefore is significantly differentiated from them. For this reason, admission numbers may prove not to be very sensitive to price after all.

Note that the price of cinema tickets can vary along the length of the demand curve, while all other factors affecting demand are held constant. A change in the price of a ticket will cause a movement along the demand curve (an extension or contraction) while a change in any of the following **conditions of demand** will shift the demand curve to the left or right (an increase or decrease of demand).

▶ **The price and closeness of substitutes** – please see the discussion in the previous section on the enduring popularity of the cinema and in the preceding point on the price of cinema tickets.

▶ **The price and closeness of complements** – the sale of complements to cinema admissions such as popcorn and soft drinks generates significant revenue for cinemas, but are unlikely to affect demand for admissions too greatly. Those deterred by the price of popcorn at the cinema can always purchase popcorn and take it in with them instead.

▶ **National income** – while national income grew considerably in the period from 1984 to 2009, there was a trend increase in cinema admissions (see Figure 17.2). If all other factors affecting cinema admissions had been constant over the period, this could be taken to suggest a positive correlation between income and cinema admissions, as is likely to be the case for most leisure pursuits (given that spending on leisure is discretionary in nature). It is interesting to note that trips to the cinema did not drop significantly below trend in the recession of the early 1990s. This casts doubt on the strength of the relationship between national income and cinema admissions.

▶ **The popularity of the films on release** – very popular films ('blockbusters') are likely to give a temporary boost to overall cinema admissions as people flock to see them. Four of the most popular films in the decade to 2007 were released in 2007 itself, boosting admissions in that year. The release of any Harry Potter film has generally increased cinema admissions in recent years (see Table 17.1).

▶ **The quality of facilities** – there has been considerable investment in cinemas in the UK in recent years, especially in the construction of multiplex cinemas (as shown in Figure 17.3). Such investment may be a response to higher demand, but improved facilities also serve to boost demand.

▶ **Advertising** – advertising is often an important way of increasing demand for a product and making it less elastic (less sensitive to price). Table 17.2 shows that £168.3 million was spent in the UK on promoting films in 2009.

Figure 17.3: Cinema screens by type 1999-2009

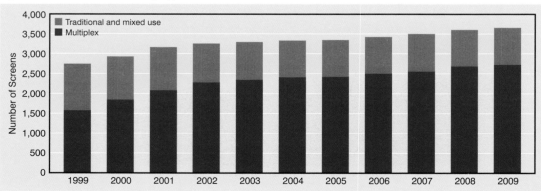

Source: UK Film Council Yearbook 2010

Table 17.1: Top 20 UK films in terms of inflation adjusted box office revenue

Title	Country of origin	UK box office total (2008/09 £ million)	UK distributor	Year of release
1 Avatar	USA	91.4*	20th Century Fox	2009
2 Titanic	USA	88.0	20th Century Fox	1998
3 Harry Potter and the Philosopher's Stone	UK/USA	79.8	Warner Bros	2001
4 Lord of the Rings: The Fellowship of the Ring	USA/NZ	76.0	Entertainment	2001
5 Mamma Mia!	UK/USA	70.9	Universal	2008
6 Jaws	USA	70.0	UIP	1975
7 Lord of the Rings: The Return of the King	USA/NZ	69.4	Entertainment	2003
8 Jurassic Park	USA	69.3	20th Century Fox	1993
9 The Full Monty	UK/USA	68.0	20th Century Fox	1997
10 Lord of the Rings: The Two Towers	USA/NZ	67.3	Entertainment	2002
11 Star Wars	USA	65.8	20th Century Fox	1977
12 Harry Potter and the Chamber of Secrets	UK/USA	64.0	Warner Bros	2002
13 Star Wars Episode 1: The Phantom Menace	USA	63.8	20th Century Fox	1999
14 Grease	USA	60.6	UIP	1978
15 Casino Royale	UK/USA/Czech	58.6	Sony Pictures	2006
16 Pirates of the Caribbean; Dead Man's Chest	USA	55.4	Buena Vista	2006
17 E.T. The Extra-Terrestrial	USA	55.2	UIP	1982
18 Toy Story 2	USA	54.7	Walt Disney	2000
19 Harry Potter and the Goblet of Fire	UK/USA	53.4	Warner Bros	2005
20 Shrek 2	USA	53.4	UIP	2004

Source: UK Film Council Statistical Yearbook 2010   *The box office gross for *Avatar* is to 4 April 2010, it was still on release at that time

Table 17.2: UK advertising spend on films 2007-09, £m

	2003	2007	2008	2009
TV	61.2	74.1	79.3	74.3
Outdoor	46.6	65.3	56.2	57.0
Press	30.1	27.0	22.6	19.9
Radio	9.7	8.4	9.4	10.7
Internet	–	4.7	4.5	6.4
Total	**147.6**	**179.5**	**172.0**	**168.3**

Source: UK Film Council Statistical Yearbook 2010

Who goes to the cinema?

Table 17.3 shows that the cinema audience was equally split between males and females. The majority of the cinema audience is young, with almost half of the total audience (49%) in 2009 being aged 24 or below. However, an interesting trend is that the proportion of older cinema-goers is increasing year-on-year. This might be explained by the fact that older people account for a greater proportion of the UK population than they used to or by the showing of more films that appeal to older people. The television audience for film is, in contrast to cinema admissions, skewed toward older viewers.

Table 17.3: Cinema audience by gender and age group 2009, %

Age	7-14	15-24	25-34	35-44	45-54	55+	Total
Male	9	15	11	8	4	3	50
Female	9	16	7	8	5	5	50
Total	**18**	**31**	**18**	**16**	**9**	**8**	**100**

Source: UK Film Council Statistical Yearbook 2010

In terms of social groupings, cinema is most popular with professionals ('AB') and higher-skilled manual workers ('C1') as shown in Table 17.4. This is probably due in part to the higher incomes enjoyed by these groups, although as noted in the section on 'Factors affecting demand for cinema admissions' there is evidence that the overall demand for the cinema is not that sensitive to national income. The higher attendance by the AB and C1 groups may also be explained by cultural factors – these groups may simply have more interest in watching films, for example.

Table 17.4: Cinema audience by social group 2009, %

	AB	C1	C2	DE	Total
Top 20 films (proportion of audience)	29	34	19	19	100
Top UK films (proportion of audience)	34	35	16	15	100
Total survey population 7+	**25**	**29**	**21**	**25**	**100**

Source: UK Film Council Statistical Yearbook 2010   Percentages may not add up to 100 due to rounding
Note: AB – Professional, business and white collar; C1 – Higher-skilled manual; C2 – Lower-skilled manual; DE – 'Semi-' and 'Un-skilled' manual

Table 17.5: Cinema screens by exhibitors with 20+ screens, 2009

	Sites	**Screens**	**% of Total Screens**
Odeon	106	840	23.0
Cineworld	76	773	21.2
Vue	67	641	17.6
National Amusements	21	274	7.5
Ward Anderson	25	213	5.8
Apollo	13	77	2.1
City Screen	18	51	1.4
Reel Cinemas	14	51	1.4
Movie House Cinemas	5	39	1.1
Merlin Cinemas	10	31	0.8
AMC	2	28	0.8
Others*	366	633	17.3
Total	**723**	**3,651**	**100.0**

Source: UK Film Council Statistical Yearbook 2010   *14 major exhibitors and 312 independent single venue exhibitors

The structure of the market for cinema admissions

The five largest cinema chains in the UK owned over 75% of all screens in 2009. This suggests that the market is an oligopoly. Twelve exhibitors owned 20 screens or more. This data is confirmed in Table 17.5.

One reason why the market is so highly concentrated is the economies of scale available to large chains. There are likely to be significant managerial economies for national chains through the employment of industry professionals and marketing economies too (a single website can handle online bookings across the entire country, for example). It is mainly national chains that have the financial muscle to build and maintain modern multiplex facilities. National chains can raise the finance for such investments more cheaply than independent cinemas and the ability to show a wide range of films in a multiplex cinema boosts audiences. Market concentration has been increased over the years through horizontal integration (merger or takeover) as national chains have sought to grow further in order to exploit the available economies of scale.

However, there is a position in the market for smaller exhibitors. The UK Film Council classifies a range of venues including independent cinemas and film societies as community cinema providers. In many cases, these providers cater for specialist interests showing films that are not being shown at the same time by national chains. Thus they are not in direct competition to the larger firms in the industry.

Pricing and competition in the market for cinema admissions

National cinema chains are unlikely to charge the same price at each of their cinemas. Prices will be set according to conditions in the local market. If in a particular town or region one company has the only multiplex cinema, they enjoy a local monopoly and the price will be higher as a result. On the other hand, where there are two or more multiplex cinemas in fairly close proximity to each other then oligopolistic conditions prevail, and competing cinemas must take account of the actions and reactions of rivals when setting price. A situation of interdependence will exist. Prices are unlikely to be as high as where there is only one cinema, but intense price competition is perhaps also unlikely as cinema chains recognise that it is not in their mutual interest to spark a price war.

Another reason why prices vary from region to region is provided by the different land prices in different areas of the country and other regional differences in costs. Table 17.6 offers a comparison of prices for Cineworld in Nottingham and the London, Fulham Road site. The land on which the cinema in London is sited is more valuable and wages of staff are doubtless higher. This helps to explain the higher prices in London.

Table 17.6 also shows that Cineworld (in common with other national chains) engages in price discrimination. Groups with relative inelastic demand, such as adults wishing to view films at peak times, pay relatively high prices. Groups with more elastic demand, such as students, pay lower prices.

Table 17.6: Admission prices at Cineworld

	Nottingham	London, Fulham Road
Adult (after 5pm Monday-Friday, all day Saturday-Sunday & bank holidays)	£8.20	£10.50
Adult (before 5pm Monday-Friday)	£6.80	£8.00
Child (14 & under)	£5.70	£6.60
Student	£5.70	£7.00
Senior Citizen	£5.70	£7.00
Family* (after 5pm, Monday-Friday, all day Saturday-Sunday & bank holidays)	£24.00	£29.00
Family* (before 5pm, Monday-Friday)	£22.00	£24.60

Source: Based on information accessed at www.cineworld.co.uk on 16th July 2011
*Family tickets cover groups of two adults with two children, or one adult and three children

It is difficult for cinemas to differentiate themselves from one another. Although there may be small differences between attending one multiplex cinema and another (such as the style of seating) the experience is essentially similar (homogeneous). This limits the scope for non-price competition, although

such competition may take place in less obvious ways. National chains may compete to secure the most lucrative locations for their cinemas, for example.

Digital cinema

A significant development in cinemas in the coming years is likely to be conversion to use digital projectors to show films. Such conversion carries a high cost, with digital projectors typically costing three or four times as much as conventional projectors and having a fraction of the lifespan. For this reason, cinemas have been reluctant to convert to digital projectors unless they can reach an agreement to share the cost of conversion with film distributors.

However, conversion to digital may offer national chains significant additional advantages on top of those they already enjoy. It is possible that the quality of films provided digitally may exceed the quality currently available. Films can be distributed to cinemas in digital form at very low cost compared to that for conventional film. Indeed, distributors may one day cease to make films available to cinemas on conventional film and this could threaten the future of cinemas unable to meet the conversion cost. Cinemas with digital projectors may also be able to use their facilities to show live sports events on a pay-per-view basis.

Spectator Sports

Sport has become increasingly business orientated in recent years, and consequently interest in it as a field for economic study has increased. The dominant sport in terms of wealth in the UK is football, with most of this wealth concentrated in the FA Premier League. This dominance is reflected in much of the material contained in this case study, but examples from a number of other sports are also drawn upon.

Objectives of sports providers

It is standard for economists to assume that the aim of the firm is to maximise profits.

Two important factors in determining whether this is so in reality are (a) who owns the firm; and (b) who controls its behaviour? It is argued that if the behaviour of the firm is controlled by people other than its owners (management and directors, for example) this may cause the firm to deviate from profit maximisation.

A particular issue concerning the objectives of sports clubs is whether they put sporting success ahead of profit. Supporters generally want sporting success to be the number one priority and, in many cases, the owners of clubs have shared this viewpoint. Chelsea FC made a loss of £140m in the year to the end of June 2005, after a loss of £87.8m in the previous year. These losses were made possible by the financial backing of the club's owner, Russian billionaire Roman Abramovich, who has been happy to bankroll the club as it won the Premiership title in both 2005 and 2006. The future of some clubs has been jeopardised by incurring costs that they can ill afford (through wages and transfer fees) in the pursuit of playing success. Leeds United and Bradford City are possible examples; there are many others.

In recent years a number of leading clubs have become 'public limited companies'. This means that the shares of the club are sold on the stock market. The advantage of this for the clubs concerned is that when new shares are first made available to the public, this provides a significant cash injection. Uses for the new funds include investment in stadiums or the acquisition of improved players. The majority of shares, however, are not purchased by fans but by financial institutions such as banks and pension funds. Financial institutions only invest in football clubs in order to receive a return on their investment: their primary interest is the profitability of the business and they put pressure on the directors of clubs to ensure that the business strategies they pursue will deliver high profits. Of course, success on the field may be important in helping a club to be profitable, because footballing success can lead to increased revenue through gate receipts, television and merchandising. Ultimately, however, success on the field is rarely pursued regardless of the cost. Consequently, fans may have to get used to star players being sold to other clubs if it makes business sense to do so, and so on.

An interesting development in the ownership of football clubs is the development of Supporter Trusts. Supporters group together to form such trusts, which are recognised by law. The aim of a Supporter Trust is usually to influence the way in which a club is run, often by acquiring shares. The ultimate aim may be for the trust to become the majority shareholder in the club, thus assuming overall control. Supporter Trusts have received financial help from the government via a scheme known as Supporters Direct. This is official recognition of the importance of football clubs to the communities in which they are based. Supporter ownership or control has been achieved at a number of clubs (such as Brentford, Chesterfield and Lincoln City). Profit maximisation is unlikely to operate at these clubs; indeed at Lincoln it is forbidden for any official or member of the club to profit from the organisation.

The market for spectator sports is heavily segmented: watching horse racing is likely to be a poor substitute for watching cricket.

Defining the market

It is open to question as to how useful it is to think in terms of a single market for spectator sports. There are a large number of spectator sports and in any one sport there might be a large number of 'producers'. Think about the large numbers of football clubs, for example. Thus, even if there is such a thing as the market for spectator sports, it is heavily segmented: watching horse racing is likely to be a poor substitute for watching cricket. Even within a particular sport, substitutability may be weak. Football fans often have a great deal of loyalty to a particular club and would not consider switching allegiance and watching another one on a regular basis instead.

While the large numbers of providers of spectator sports might initially lead to thinking of the market in terms of monopolistic competition, the differentiation within the market is too strong to make this useful. There may in fact be very substantial monopoly power for some providers of spectator sports, able to charge high prices with little fear of losing their customers to competitors. In fact, the greatest competition for some providers of spectator sports may come from outside of the market. If admission prices are too high, the fan of a particular sport or club may choose other leisure pursuits more readily than switching to other sports providers.

Another complicating factor in discussing the market for spectator sports is that some degree of cooperation is often necessary between different providers in order for there to be a product at all. In team sports, for example, it is necessary to have other teams to play against and cooperation to form leagues and cup competitions is common. The league or cup may then become a brand which is an important part of the marketing strategies of all of the competitors within it (consider for example the Barclays Premiership in football or the Twenty-20 Cup in cricket).

Admission prices

As explained in the previous section, substitutability between different providers of spectator sports is likely to be weak. This means that **demand** will be inelastic for the product of any particular provider.

Competition is unlikely to exert significant downward pressure on prices, and prices may then be higher than they would otherwise be as a result. Certainly, elasticity of demand is an important factor in pricing decisions for spectator sports. Football clubs, for example, have often charged higher prices to away fans than home fans. This makes sense, as fans who are sufficiently loyal to their clubs to travel to away matches are unlikely to be put off by an admission price raised by a pound or two.

Figure 18.1: Market conditions for a sell-out game at a leading Premier League club

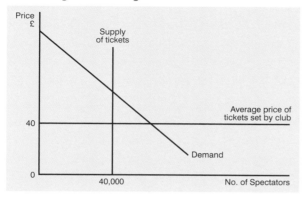

The **supply** of tickets for any given sports fixture can be regarded as being completely inelastic, at a quantity determined by the number of seats available in the stadium. While prices may seem very high for major sporting attractions such as Premiership football and test match cricket, these prices are in fact often below the equilibrium price. This is shown by the fact that many matches are 'sell-outs' and there is a greater demand for tickets at the price set than there are seats available. The price charged is effectively a **maximum price** or price ceiling. This pricing strategy may be evidence of a desire to keep the tickets affordable to genuine fans and necessitates some form of ticket rationing other than by price. Such forms of rationing include first-come-first served (queuing), a limited number of tickets per customer, lucky ballot or giving preference to regular customers (members of county cricket clubs may get privileged access to test match tickets, for example). Figure 18.1 represents market conditions for a sell-out Premier League football match, but could be adapted to show the market for any 'sell-out' sports fixture.

Matches when there are spare seats also make interesting case studies. Spare seats are common at football matches in lower leagues and for many other sports fixtures. They may become increasingly common at Premier League matches as the recession that began in 2008 bites. There is essentially no marginal cost to a club when it sells a spare seat. It should therefore be willing to sell spare seats at any price as long as this increases revenue. However, when the price is reduced to sell extra seats, the price is reduced for all seats, including those which would have been filled at a higher price. Because demand tends to be inelastic, revenue falls when price is cut, even though more seats are filled.

Figure 18.1 could also be adapted to represent the market for tickets for the London 2012 Olympic Games. With 23 million ticket applications having been made, there was a vast excess demand for tickets at the prices charged, with the result that tickets were rationed by lucky ballot. See the section in this chapter for more detail on the economics of the Olympics.

Sources of revenue

While gate receipts from the admission fees paid by spectators are a vital source of revenue in sport, other forms of revenue are increasingly important. Perhaps the most notable of these is sponsorship. Examples of this include shirt sponsorship or commercial sponsorship of competitions such as the Guinness Premiership in rugby. Increasingly, sports events have a number of commercial 'partners' whose logos are displayed behind players in post-match interviews. The total value of sports sponsorship in the UK now exceeds £1 billion annually.

Other important sources of revenue include advertising, for example advertising hoardings around the perimeter of pitches; television revenue; and the sale of merchandise, such as replica football kits. In December 2005, Umbro concluded a deal thought to be worth around £200m of revenue to the Football Association. The cornerstone of the deal is that Umbro will continue to manufacture the England kit until 2014.

Television revenues

The value of televised sport, especially live sport, has increased dramatically in recent years. This has been driven largely by the entry of new broadcasters into the television market, which has increased competition in the bidding process for the rights to televise sport. Of particular importance was the entry of BSkyB in 1988.

The development of television technology, such as digital television, has increased capacity to allow many more hours of televised sport than was previously possible. Further, many of the new channels provided are only available to those willing to pay for them. The opportunity to charge a substantial monthly fee for a sports channel, or even in some cases to charge to watch a particular match or event on a one-off 'pay-per-view' basis has made the rights to televise sport extremely valuable. This is especially the case if those rights are exclusive, so that the match or event can only be watched on a single channel.

The biggest beneficiary of increased television revenues for sport in the UK has been the FA Premiership. From 1992, BSkyB has been willing to pay huge sums in order to dominate the broadcasting of live Premiership action, enjoying exclusivity from then until the end of the 2006-07 season. This exclusivity has been the main selling point for the 'Sky Sports' channels, demand for which has been fuelled by football's popularity and growing incomes and prosperity (demand for Sky Sports is likely to be income elastic).

The total value of contracts to broadcast live matches is £1.782 billion for the three year period beginning with the 2010-11 season. For this period, Sky's exclusive possession of rights has been broken (see following section on 'Monopoly selling of television rights'). However, Sky will still broadcast the majority of the 138 matches to be shown. Table 18.1 shows how the value of top division football television rights has escalated. It is worth noting that the substantial increase in the value of rights for the 2007-08 season onwards is partly accounted for by the fact that the rights now include the entitlement to transmit on platforms such as broadband internet, not just television.

Table 18.1: The cost of rights to live top division football matches in England

Year in which season(s) began	Cost of rights per season in million £		Owner of live game rights	Real cost per live game	Number of live games per season
	Nominal	Real			
1983	2.6	3.1	ITV/BBC	0.310	10
1988	11.0	10.38	ITV	0.577	18
1992	35.5	25.67	BSkyB	0.421	61
1996	39.5	28.56	BSkyB	0.468	61
1997	182.5	111.42	BSkyB	1.826	61
2000	177.5	108.06	BSkyB	1.715	63
2004,05,06	368.3	Unavailable	BSkyB	Unavailable	138
2007,08,09	564.0	Unavailable	BSkyB/Setanta	Unavailable	138
2010,11,12	594.0	Unavailable	BSkyB/ESPN	Unavailable	138

Source: Market definition in European sports broadcasting and competition for sports broadcasting rights – a study for DGIV of the European Commission by David Harbord, Angel Hernando and Georg Von Graevenittz (available to download free of charge at www.market-analysis.co.uk); figures for 2004 onwards are derived by the author from various sources.

As more and more money has been paid by broadcasters to televise sport, so the influence of television on the nature of sport itself has increased. The scheduling of fixtures in accordance with the preferences of television viewers is an obvious example. This explains the move of Rugby League from being a winter sport to a summer one, and why many Premiership fixtures kick-off on a Sunday. In some cases, the way the game is actually played has been changed. For example, there are now many more one-day cricket matches played than before and 2003 saw the advent of the Twenty-20 Cup (only 20 overs per side), although these changes appear to suit spectators actually attending matches as well as the television audience.

In football, it can be argued that the game has become less competitive, as those clubs receiving the greatest shares of the television money have been able increasingly to command the top players through high wages and transfer fees. This has meant that there are only a handful of clubs with a realistic chance of actually winning the league. This is reflected in Table 18.2. The majority of earnings shown in the table are derived from television and the four biggest earning clubs are some distance ahead of the others. Arsenal, first in the earnings table, had earnings more than double those of fifth-placed Tottenham. Between 1995 and 2011, only three clubs won the FA Premiership (Arsenal, Chelsea and Manchester United).

*Table 18.2: Earnings, in £m, by Premier League clubs in 2005-06 season
(not including gate receipts or merchandise income)*

	Premiership	Europe	Cups	Total
Arsenal	27.2	25.1	0.4	52.7
Chelsea	28.6	17.7	1.2	47.5
Liverpool	28.1	12.7	3.4	44.2
Manchester Utd	29.1	9.8	0.9	39.8
Tottenham	25.9	N/a	0.3	26.2
West Ham	22.3	N/a	2.1	24.4
Middlesbrough	19.3	4.0	1.0	24.3
Newcastle	23.2	N/a	0.8	24.0
Bolton	22.0	1.0	0.7	23.7
Blackburn	23.4	N/a	0.2	23.6
Wigan	22.7	N/a	0.2	22.9
Everton	22.2	Negligible	0.2	22.4
Charlton	20.1	N/a	0.9	21.0
Man City	19.7	N/a	0.9	20.6
Fulham	20.1	N/a	0.2	20.3
Aston Villa	18.9	N/a	0.7	19.6
Birmingham	18.6	N/a	0.8	19.4
Portsmouth	17.7	N/a	0.3	18.0
West Bromwich	16.7	N/a	0.2	16.9
Sunderland	15.9	N/a	0.2	16.1

Premier League earnings: Prize money: max £9.7m, min £485,000; TV cash: £9m per club plus £340,000 or £250,000 for each live Sky game, depending on timing and whether a pay per view game;

Overseas TV, sponsorship and licensing money: £4m per club.

European: Champions League earnings: TV money and performance bonuses; Uefa Cup: sums estimated as clubs sell own TV and sponsorship rights.

FA Cup: Prize money: £40,000 for third round win rising to £1m for final win; TV money: £150,000 to £265,000 per live match.

Carling Cup: £100,000 for clubs in a live televised match.

Source: *The Independent*, Thursday 11th May 2006

Sport and competition law

There have been a number of high profile competition cases involving sport, and in particular football in recent years.

▶ Monopoly selling of television rights

The clubs of the FA Premiership currently sell rights to broadcast matches collectively. They act effectively as a joint monopoly, rather than each club competing to sell the rights to its home games individually. The

effect of this monopoly is to reduce supply (until 2004-05 only around 60 out of 380 matches per season were televised) and raise the price paid for televised football. Further, live Premiership football has only been available from a single broadcaster, BSkyB, since 1992. In 1999, the Office of Fair Trading brought a monopoly case against the FA Premier League to the Restrictive Practices Court. The League defended itself on the basis that were clubs to negotiate individually with television companies, a huge gulf in income between clubs would be created. For example, the value of Manchester United games would vastly exceed that of Bolton Wanderers matches. This would reduce the attractiveness of the League, because smaller clubs would be less able to compete effectively. Ultimately, the survival of smaller clubs may be threatened and a breakaway of the larger clubs to compete against clubs of a similar size in Europe would be likely. A further point is that the current arrangements allow consumers the convenience of accessing the matches of all clubs on a single television channel. The Court ruled that the current arrangements did not operate against the **public interest**, and thus no action was taken against the Premier League.

In recent years the theme of the monopoly power exercised by Premiership clubs has been taken up by the European Commission. The FA has been forced to divide matches into six packages of 23 matches per season as from the 2007-08 season, with the requirement that no single broadcaster can be awarded all six packages. As a result, BSkyB's monopoly has been broken and for the three seasons from 2010-11, ESPN has won the rights to one of the packages, a total of 23 matches. However, Sky has won the rights to the most attractive package of matches, to be broadcast late on Sunday afternoons and remains dominant. It has even been suggested that of all the broadcasters who engaged in the bidding process, ESPN was BSkyB's preferred recipient of any packages it did not itself win. Other broadcasters, especially free-to-air broadcasters such as the BBC and ITV, would have provided a much greater threat to BSkyB's position. In many respects, this outcome is the nearest to the continuation of Sky's monopoly permissible under the new rules.

▶ Mobility of labour

The single market of the European Union provides for the completely free movement of goods, services and factors of production (including labour) between member states of the Union. In the 'Bosman Case' of 1995, the European Court of Justice ruled that the practice of football clubs charging a transfer fee for players was a restriction on the freedom of movement of footballers. This was acceptable while a player was still under contract to his club, but illegal when a player's contract had expired. Since this case, players have been able to move anywhere in Europe on a 'free transfer' at the end of their contracts. An exception to this has been allowed for players under the age of 24, in order to encourage clubs to invest in the development of young players.

The Bosman ruling is one of the forces leading to higher salaries for footballers, as clubs may now spend money on wages that they previously would have paid in transfer fees. Demand for footballers at any given salary level has also been buoyed by the vast revenues coming into the game (for example from television and sponsorship). This is combined with a strictly limited and inelastic supply of players of sufficient quality to play football at a high level.

The Bosman ruling means that clubs may now spend money on wages that they previously would have paid in transfer fees.

▶ BSkyB and Manchester United

In 1999, the Secretary of State for Trade and Industry blocked a proposed merger between BSkyB and Manchester United FC on the recommendation of the Competition Commission. The merger would have been an example of vertical integration with BSkyB being one step forward from Manchester United in the supply chain of televised football. The Competition Commission found three distinct threats posed by the merger to the **public interest**. (i) The merger would enhance BSkyB's ability to secure the Premier League television rights in the future. This would act as a barrier to entry, restricting the entry into the premium sports channel market by other providers; (ii) it would reinforce the trend towards greater inequality of wealth between clubs, thus weakening the smaller ones; (iii) it would give BSkyB additional influence over Premier League decisions relating to the organisation of football, leading to some decisions which did not reflect the long term interests of football. The Competition Commission found no public interest benefits of the merger.

▶ Sale of replica kits

In 2003 the sportswear manufacturer Umbro was found guilty by the Office of Fair Trading of acting with the Football Association, Manchester United and a number of sportswear retailers (including JJB) to fix the prices of replica football kits at artificially high levels. This was in breach of the Competition Act of 1998, and heavy penalties were imposed on the parties concerned.

Replica kits affected included those of England and Manchester United. Umbro had withheld supply of kits to retailers wishing to sell them at below the retailers recommended price, thus preventing price competition between different stores on the sale of shirts. Since this ruling, the price of replica shirts has fallen considerably.

There is little doubt that the market for Umbro kits is more competitive following the ruling. Table 18.3 suggests that customers may be able to make considerable savings by shopping around for the best price when buying an England shirt. In the run up to the 2006 World Cup it was possible to buy a white England 'home' shirt for as little as £9.99. The enormous volume of sales that resulted contrasts sharply with the restricted supply, high price outcome of the collective monopoly that had operated under the price-fixing agreement. However, some concerns remain. These include the fact that shirts for children are in many cases discounted only marginally from the adult price. Further, some retailers remain expensive. A lack of information may lead consumers to pay more than double the price charged by the cheapest retailer.

Table 18.3: Prices charged by different retailers for a red England 'away' shirt

	Adult shirt	**Child shirt**
FA	£22.49	£17.49
JJB Sports	£29.00	£24.00
Kitbag	£39.99	£29.99
Littlewoods	£35.00	£30.00
M and M Direct	£19.66	£19.66
Sportsworld	£44.99	£34.99
Streetwise Sports	£25.00	£20.00
Subside Sports	£39.99	£36.99

Source: *The Times*, Thursday 1st June 2006, using figures from *Which?* based on online price

▶ Rugby

Competition law has also affected other sports besides football. For example in 2003, intervention by the Office of Fair Trading led to a change of rules for promotion to Rugby's Zurich Premiership. It was thought anti-competitive that clubs should be denied promotion on the basis that they were not the main tenant of their home stadium, a ruling which had denied promotion to Rotherham RUFC in 2001/02. The rule was changed such that the only requirement of clubs was to provide a suitable venue on the fixture dates specified by the league.

The cost of constructing the London Olympic facilities comes from central government, the National Lottery and London's Council tax payers.

Spectator sports and government funding

Government funding for sport may be justified on the grounds that sport is a **merit good**, carrying greater social benefits than private benefits (**positive externalities**) and would thus be under-provided in a free market. However, this argument applies more clearly to participation in sport (where there are health benefits and thus a reduced burden on the NHS) than it does to spectator sports. While there are some positive externalities from spectator sports (such as the general value of a football club to its local community), government has tended to see spectator sports as private commercial enterprises which must stand on their own feet.

On occasion, public (government) funding may be judged appropriate for spectator-sports related investment provided that there are clear social benefits.

There are examples of large stadium investments acting to encourage further investment. For example, the £750 million redevelopment of Wembley Stadium is seen as the stimulus for the upgrading of the nearby underground station. This creates a possible case for public funding – the Department for Culture, Media and Sport is providing £20 million towards the project – but this is the exception rather than the rule. While most stadium building carries some beneficial **multiplier effects** for the local economy, these may be small and difficult to quantify and the projects would therefore have to be financed commercially or through grants from bodies such as the Football Trust. More substantial government funding is to be provided for the London 2012 Olympics (please see next section).

The London 2012 Olympic Games – costs and benefits

The cost of constructing Olympic facilities and regenerating the Lower Lea Valley area in London is estimated at £5.6bn, although an announcement in March 2007 allocated a total budget of £9.3bn to include a contingency fund to be used in the event that costs exceed the estimate. The money comes from central government, the National Lottery and London's Council tax payers. The £2bn cost of staging the games once the facilities have been built will be met though the sale of television rights, corporate sponsorship and ticket sales. These sources of revenue, especially television and sponsorship, have become more important in recent Games, as shown in Table 18.4.

Table 18.4: Olympic Games revenue sources Munich 1972-Beijing 2008

	Munich 1972	Montreal 1976	Los Ang. 1984	Seoul 1988	Barcelona 1992	Atlanta 1996	Sydney 2000	Beijing 2008
Others	40.4	44.7	261.6	136.7	313.6	169.7	2.6	326.0
Lottery	203.5	481.6	0	183.6	195.4	0	0	180.0
Stamps	3.1	20.5	0	6.5	7.3	0	0	12.0
Coins	735.0	219.0	52.5	187.2	56.3	14.6	13.1	8.0
Donations	0	0	0	170.0	119.0	0	0	20.0
Tickets	58.5	56.6	227.6	37.0	91.7	416.6	444.9	140.0
Merchandising	4.1	5.8	21.9	23.3	14.9	72.4	47.8	N/A
Sponsoring	0	40.3	219.0	245.5	549.5	587.7	605.2	330.0
Television	40.0	70.9	340.4	358.4	488.5	555.4	678.9	709.0

Source: http://olympics.pthimon.co.uk/micro2.htm

Table 18.5: Costs and benefits of the London 2012 Olympics

Costs	Benefits
Construction of facilities and regeneration of the Lower Lea Valley area: £5.6 bn* (the government has allocated a budget of £9.3bn including a contingency fund of £2.7bn; of this £9.3bn, £6bn comes from the government, £2.2bn from the National Lottery and £1.1bn from London's council tax payers)	· Employment in construction facilities · Boost to tourism · Economic regeneration of the Lower Lea Valley · Temporary boost to consumption during the Games · Multiplier effects from additional government spending
Staging of the games: £2bn* (to be raised through selling of television rights, corporate sponsorship and ticket sales) Employment in construction facilities	· Social benefits from the use of Olympic facilities by local sports clubs after the Games, and the housing accommodation provided by the Olympic Village

*Based on government estimates of costs announced in March 2007

The principle of opportunity cost should be used in evaluating the effects shown in Table 18.5. Do the benefits of the games exceed the benefits that could be derived from spending the money elsewhere? For example, the £2.2bn contribution from the National Lottery diverts money from other good causes that it funds. Which is the better use of the money? Money from central government and London's taxpayers may be diverted from other areas such as education or healthcare.

Television Broadcasting

The most popular leisure pursuit in the UK

"Television viewing is the most popular leisure pursuit by far in the UK. At any one time of the evening, as much as 44% of the population can be sitting in front of a TV set. On average, more time is devoted to watching television than is spent reading, listening to the radio, playing sport and socialising combined. This is true across the age spectrum, from children to those over 65." (www.ofcom.org.uk/consultations/Whatpeoplewatch). A reflection of this popularity is that total revenue for the television industry exceeded £11.2bn in 2007.

Terrestrial television

Technological developments have led to rapid change in the television broadcasting market in recent years. The traditional method of receiving television channels was via an *analogue signal*, received through a roof-top aerial. The analogue spectrum only had the capacity to broadcast a strictly limited number of channels. As a result the television market was inevitably **oligopolistic**, with very high barriers to entry. The chief amongst these was the need for a licence from the government to use one of the small number of positions available on the analogue spectrum. Entries into the market were very rare indeed, the traditional three-channel set up (BBC1, BBC2, ITV) being added to only by Channel 4 (1982) and Five (1997). Collectively, the five stations have come to be known as *'terrestrial television channels'*.

Within this oligopoly, there was no scope for **price competition**. This was because all channels were made available 'free to air'. ITV (and later Channel 4 and Five) had to fund their programming and seek to make profit from the revenue gained by selling advertising space in breaks between and during programmes. The BBC is a classic example of a *public service broadcaster* and is funded through the licence fees that all television viewers have to pay in order to be allowed to own and watch a television.

Table 19.1: The BBC as a public service broadcaster – Characteristics of BBC programming, as required in the renewal of its charter to cover the period 1st January 2007 to 31st December 2016

The BBC should provide a wide range of content, across every genre, trying to reach the greatest possible range of audiences. Where possible, it should make subjects accessible to new audiences. Its programmes should set standards, especially in news, for other broadcasters to aspire to.

Programmes should aim to be excellent, distinctive and entertaining – that means, more specifically, that they should be:
· Of high quality
· Challenging
· Original
· Innovative
· Engaging

Every programme should display at least one of the above characteristics of excellence and distinctiveness.

Source: Department for Culture, Media and Sport, White Paper, 'A public service for all: The BBC in the digital age'

As a public service broadcaster the BBC is charged with providing education, information and entertainment for all. This implies a diverse range of programming and its goals are not primarily commercial (see Table 19.1). Nevertheless there is clear evidence of competition for audience share between the BBC and ITV.

For ITV, viewing figures are especially important, because these determine the value of the advertising slots through which the network obtains its revenue. It is possible to argue that the funding available to the BBC and the consequent quality of its programming has forced ITV to invest heavily in quality home-produced programmes, including drama and comedy. This argument was amongst those deployed by the BBC in its successful bid for the renewal of its charter for 2007-2016. In essence, the argument claims that the existence of the BBC leads to competition on the quality of programming, and that this is to the benefit of all.

Figure 19.1: Audience shares, 1982-2009

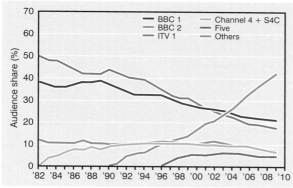

Source: The Communications Market 2010 (Ofcom)

Figure 19.1 shows a downward trend in audience share for both BBC1 and ITV since 1982. The decline in ITV's audience share has been particularly pronounced since alternatives to the terrestrial channels became available in 1991. This suggests that the channels newly available since 1991 are closer substitutes for the programmes broadcast by ITV than they are for the programme content of BBC1.

The changing market for television

The rapid advance of technology has vastly increased choice for consumers in the market for television. The most significant of these choices is perhaps the choice of a *platform* (method of receiving signals) for viewing. Besides the traditional method of receiving analogue signals through a television aerial (which is to be phased out by 2012) it is now possible to receive *digital television signals* through one of three platforms: satellite television; digital terrestrial television, e.g. through a set-top box; and through cable television.

Digital television signals can be received through satellite television, digital terrestrial television or cable television.

Figure 19.2: The UK television market

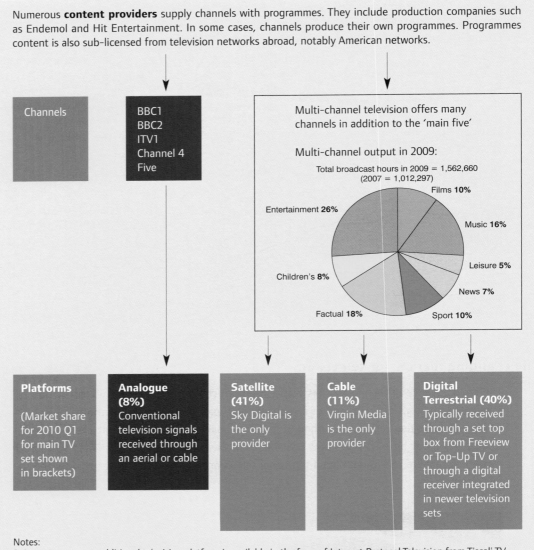

Numerous **content providers** supply channels with programmes. They include production companies such as Endemol and Hit Entertainment. In some cases, channels produce their own programmes. Programmes content is also sub-licensed from television networks abroad, notably American networks.

| Channels | BBC1
BBC2
ITV1
Channel 4
Five | Multi-channel television offers many channels in addition to the 'main five'

Multi-channel output in 2009:
Total broadcast hours in 2009 = 1,562,660
(2007 = 1,012,297)

Films 10%, Music 16%, Entertainment 26%, Leisure 5%, Children's 8%, News 7%, Factual 18%, Sport 10% |

| **Platforms**

(Market share for 2010 Q1 for main TV set shown in brackets) | **Analogue (8%)**
Conventional television signals received through an aerial or cable | **Satellite (41%)**
Sky Digital is the only provider | **Cable (11%)**
Virgin Media is the only provider | **Digital Terrestrial (40%)**
Typically received through a set top box from Freeview or Top-Up TV or through a digital receiver integrated in newer television sets |

Notes:
1. In some areas, an additional television platform is available in the form of Internet Protocol Television from Tiscali TV.
2. From 2008 analogue TV signals will be turned off on a region-by-region basis. By 2012, analogue signals will not be available anywhere in the UK and the 'digital switchover' will be complete.
3. Digital platforms are shown in green.

Source: Constructed using official CPI weights quoted in *Consumer Prices Index and Retail Prices Index: Updating Weights for 2010,* Sharne Bailey, Prices Division, Office for National Statistics

The distinctive feature of digital television is that the signals are compressed in such a way that the digital spectrum can carry many television channels, whereas the analogue spectrum could support only a few. This means that viewers who have chosen to view through a digital platform have a huge choice of channels. This choice varies little from one digital platform to another although the combinations in which the different platforms bundle channels into packages *does* vary. Viewers pay a monthly subscription charge for each package of channels that they choose and may also have the opportunity to make a one-off payment (*'pay-per-view'*) to watch films and major sporting events.

Competition between platforms

By early 2010, 92.1% of UK homes had access to multi-channel television (see Figure 19.3 for more details), viewing on a digital platform in most cases. The UK government has the intention of turning off the analogue signal in 2012, forcing all households to receive their television channels through a digital platform.

Figure 19.3: Multi-channel penetration in the UK

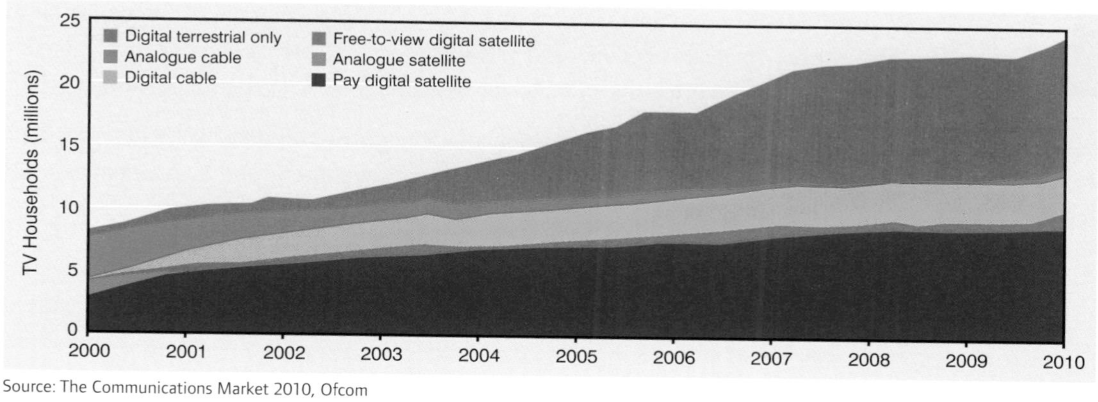

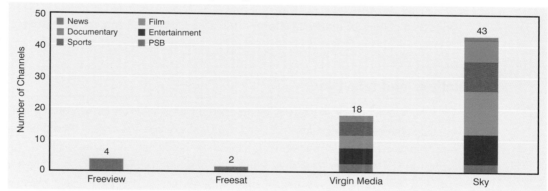

Source: The Communications Market 2010, Ofcom

With three platforms available, the platform market can be characterised as **oligopolistic**. While there are some attempts at product differentiation, in truth the services offered through each platform are similar. The range of channels available does not vary much from one platform to another and there is increasingly wide availability on all platforms of additional services such as on-demand programming, high definition signals and the facility to pause and rewind live television.

There is significant scope for price competition between platforms, especially for recruiting new subscribers, who tend to be fairly loyal once they have chosen their platform and may therefore generate revenue streams for years to come. Existing subscribers tend to be unaware of the prices of other platform providers or are unwilling to go to the inconvenience of switching platforms. The best deals may therefore be reserved for new digital subscribers or those willing to switch platforms.

The growing market for HD television is providing a new focus for competition between platforms. Cable and satellite platforms currently offer many more HD channels than alternative platforms for digital signals, as shown in Figure 19.4.

Figure 19.4: HD Channels by availability and genre 2010

Source: The Communications Market, 2010

Monopolistic competition between channels?

As shown in Figure 19.2 there is a wide range of channels to choose from. It is possible that competition between channels in today's television market could be modelled in terms of **monopolistic competition**. Such a market has free entry and a large number of slightly differentiated products.

It is certainly true that there are a great number of very similar channels available (37 shopping channels, for example!), although in many cases one media group may own a number of channels. Barriers to entry to new channels have also been considerably reduced by the new technology of the digital spectrum, making it possible for hundreds of channels to co-exist. New technology may also serve to reduce the

investment in capital equipment required to launch a new channel. Providers of new channels do not need to invest heavily in programming content. Many of the channels available on digital source their content cheaply from American networks and repeats; where new programmes are made directly by or for the new channels, these are often ones which are cheap to produce, such as quiz shows.

If this analysis is broadly correct, freedom of entry (**contestability**) will lead to a situation in which owners of television channels make little, if any, supernormal profit and an economically efficient outcome is achieved.

But is there really freedom of entry (contestability)?

While the digital age has undoubtedly reduced many barriers to entry, it should be noted that some sizeable ones still remain. Among these is the fact that there are large economies of scale available. The costs of providing television channels are mostly fixed: they do not alter if a million viewers tune into a programme rather than just a thousand. This means that to achieve low average costs, it is necessary to secure large numbers of viewers. In a market where the audience is already spread thinly between many channels, this is difficult to achieve. In fact, this points to the possibility of **integration** leading to a more **concentrated market** in the future, with fewer channels, but more viewers per channel.

Further, in digital media, content can easily be transferred between formats. There may be considerable cost advantages available to multi-media firms providing not just television, but other media services, such as web-site content, newspapers and digital radio. These cost advantages are examples of **economies of scope**.

Entry into the market to offer 'high quality' programme content to rival that of the BBC and ITV would be especially difficult. This is due to the high cost of producing quality programmes, which at present is actually rising as the increased number of global multi-media companies are generating increased competition for services of skilled professionals who are in short supply.

All of this suggests that the television market is less contestable than it might at first appear and that it may actually become less competitive (more concentrated) in the future. To the extent that digital television *does* create and encourage competition, this may prove to be in cheap, 'low quality', programming. This suggests a danger of **market failure** in the absence of **government regulation** of the market for television.

Externalities and television

Watching television may sometimes be associated with significant **externalities**. Too many hours spent watching television, for example, may lead to lack of exercise and obesity. Resulting health problems may then require expensive NHS treatment, imposing a burden on the tax payer, who is a third party to the original act of watching television. Further, it is sometimes held that watching television influences behaviour in ways that have a negative influence on society. Watching violent films or pornography may fall into this category, but this is a subjective and contentious issue. One concern, however, is that multi-channel television may make it more difficult to prevent children accessing such material.

Against such concerns should be set any positive externalities from watching television. These may include the beneficial effects to third parties of individuals receiving information and education through watching television. There may also be benefits of social bonding through mass watching of big television events, such as major sports matches involving national teams.

Markets take no account of externalities. Consumers and producers of television can only be expected to take into account their own **private costs and benefits** when making decisions about purchasing and supplying television programmes. This creates the possibility of market failure through allocative inefficiency and further reinforces the case for careful regulation of the television market.

Television signals as public goods

Public goods possess two key characteristics. They are **non-rivalrous**, in that consumption by one person does not leave any less of the good for others to consume. They are also **non-excludable**, so that once they have been provided no-one can be prevented from enjoying their benefits. These characteristics are at the root of the **free-rider problem**: each individual has an incentive not to pay, hoping to enjoy the benefits resulting from payments made by others. This may lead to market failure through a lack of provision of public goods, as it would be difficult to make a profit through supplying them.

Television signals are *not* pure public goods. They *can* be provided for a profit because they are excludable. The scrambling of signals and the need for a decoder, for instance, can deny access to those who have not paid for a particular channel.

However, television signals *are* **quasi-public goods**. They *do* possess the characteristic of non-rivalry: if an extra person tunes into a particular programme, this does not prevent those already watching from continuing to enjoy it. This means that the average costs of supplying television programmes may fall almost indefinitely as more and more viewers watch any given programme. Consequently, it may be **productively inefficient** to have small numbers of viewers watching a particular programme.

In terms of **allocative efficiency**, the marginal cost of providing a television programme to an extra viewer may be zero. Remembering that the condition for the attainment of allocative efficiency is that price should be set equal to marginal cost, this would imply an efficient price of zero. This is one reason why the government is keen to support free-to-air television channels provided through digital platforms, although viewers have to pay for the platform itself. A further reason for continuing to support free-to-air television is the wish that key channels should be affordable to everyone, an equity consideration. Not withstanding this, premium services such as sport and movies are always likely to carry substantial subscription fees.

Index

Absolute poverty 67
Activity rates 3
Admission prices 94-95
Advertising 88-89
Ageing population 56-59
Air travel 83-86
Allocative efficiency 74, 107
Analogue television 104

Barriers to entry 102
Bosman ruling 98
Brain drain 59

Cable television 103-106
Child Tax Credit 71
Cinema 87-92
Claimant count 42
Closed shop 28, 29
Collective bargaining 28
Collusion 76-78
Compensating differential 20
Competitive labour market
    16-19
Concentrated market 106
Concentration ratio 72
Consumer surplus 74
Contestability 83, 106
Cross-price elasticity of
    demand 85

David Ricardo 17
Deadweight welfare loss 74
Deciles 61
Demand management 54
Demographic timebomb 4, 56
Demographics 6, 59
Dependency ratios 57
Derived demand 11
Digital television 103-106
Digital terrestrial television
    103-106
Disabilities 8
Discrimination 24, 27, 43
Distribution of income and
    wealth 60-63
Dominant strategy 77

Economic and Monetary Union
    (EMU) 52
Economic inactivity 3
Economic Rent 17, 19
Economies of scope 106
Education and training 47-48
Effective marginal tax rates 69
Elasticity of demand for labour
    14-15
Elasticity of labour supply 9
Employment pattern 11
Enterprise Zones 54
Entry barriers 72, 78, 83-84
Entry-limit pricing 78
Environment 86
Ethnic groups 7-8, 27, 43
EU labour market legislation 52
Eurozone 52
External costs 38
Externalities 106

Factors of production 1
Fairness at Work 34
Female participation ratio 3, 6-7
Fixed costs 82
Flow concept 60
Football 96-97
Free-rider problem 107
Freedom of entry 106

Game theory 77
Gender pay gap 22-24
Geographical immobility of
    labour 39
Gini coefficient 65-66
Glass ceiling 24
Government funding 100
Government intervention 34-37
Government regulation 106

HD television 105
Holidays and leisure travel 79-86
Horizontal integration 85
Human capital 36

Immigration 47
Inactivity rates 3
Incentive to work 35
Income 60
Income and substitution
    effects 8-9
Income redistribution 64
Indirect taxation 71
Industrial disputes 31
Inequality and poverty 67-71
Inequality measurement 64-66
Integration 85, 106
Interdependence 76

Job Seeker's Allowance (JSA)
    38, 48
Joint monopoly 76-77
Labour Demand 11-15
Labour flexibility 29
Labour force 3-5
Labour Force Survey 43
Labour market by gender 2
Labour market flexibility 50-55
Labour mobility 44, 48-50
Labour supply 3-10
Law of diminishing marginal
    returns 12
Legislation 34-35
Leisure markets 2
Lifetime earnings 22
Local labour markets 1
London 2012 Olympic Games
    100-101
Lorenz curve 64, 65

Maastricht Treaty 52
Male participation ratios 7
Marginal physical product (MPP)
    12-13
Marginal productivity theory
    12-15
Marginal revenue (MR) 13
Marginal revenue product (MRP)
    13-14, 20, 25, 33

Marginal revenue productivity 20
Market failure 106
Maximum price 95
Means-tested benefits 58, 68-69
Median hourly pay 22
Merit good 100
Minimum wage 35-37
Mobility of labour 98
Monopolistic competition 73, 76,
    105-106
Monopoly 73-75
Monopsonist power 25
Monopsony 32-33
Multiplier effects 100

Natural rate of unemployment
    39-40
Negative externality 86
New Deal 48-49, 70-71
Non-Accelerating Inflation Rate
    of Unemployment (NAIRU)
    39, 50
Non-excludable 107
Non-price competition 78
Non-rivalrous 107
Normal profits 72, 78
North-south divide 26

Occupational immobility of
    labour 39
Occupational labour markets 1
Oligopolistic 102, 105
Oligopoly 73, 76-78
Opportunity cost 8, 17

Package holidays 79-81
Part-time work 23
Participation ratios 3, 5-8
Pay-per-view 104
Pensions 57
Percentiles 61
Perfect competition 73-75
Perfect mobility 20
Population of working age 3
Positive externalities 100
Poverty 67-71
Poverty trap 68
Price competition 76, 102
Price discrimination 75-76
Price mechanism 82
Price taker 13
Price war 76
Price-takers 72
Primary sector 11
Private costs and benefits 106
Productive efficiency 74
Productively inefficient 107
Productivity 44, 46
Progressive tax system 64, 65, 70
Public goods 107
Public interest 98-99

Quasi-public goods 107
Quasi-rent 19
Quaternary sector 11
Quintiles 61

Real unit labour costs 44

Regional policy 54-55
Regional Selective Assistance
    (RSA) 54
Regressive taxation 71
Relative poverty 67
Replacement levels 56
Replacement ratio 69
Replica kits 99
Revenue 95-97
Rugby 99

Satellite television 103-106
Secondary picketing 29
Secondary sector 11
Secret ballots 29
Short run 12
Skills 45-48
Skills shortages 45
Social Chapter 52
Social exclusion 67
Spectator sports 93-101
Sport and competition law 97-99
Sports providers 93-94
Stock concept 60
Structural change 11
Sunk costs 78, 82
Supernormal profit 72, 74
Supply chain 87
Supply-side policies 29, 54

Target income 9
Tax base 58
Technological advance 12
Television audience shares 103
Television broadcasting 102-107
Television revenues 96-97
Television rights 97-98
Terrestrial television 102
Tertiary sector 11
Time lags 18
Tour operators 80-81
Trade unions 28-33
Transfer earnings 17, 19

Unemployed 3
Unemployment 38-43
Unemployment trap 35, 68
Unemployment, Classical 38
Unemployment, frictional 39
Unemployment, Keynesian 38
Unemployment, search 39
Unemployment, seasonal 39
Unemployment, structural 39
Union density 29-30
Union mark-up 29
Union membership 30
Unit labour costs 44
Universal benefits 58, 68-69

Voluntary unemployment 36

Wage determination 16-19
Wage differentials 20-27, 61
Wages 13, 28-29
Wealth 60
Work force 3
Working population 3, 6
Working Tax Credit (WTC) 70